Fodor's InFocus

GRAND CANYON NATIONAL PARK

T0104122

Welcome to Grand Canyon National Park

Formed by the Colorado River over an estimated 2,000 million years, the Grand Canyon cuts 277 miles through northern Arizona. It's one of the Seven Natural Wonders of the World, but it's more than just a sight to see, offering adventures from air tours to zip-lining. As you plan your upcoming travels to the Grand Canyon, please confirm that places are still open and let us know when we need to make updates by emailing editors@fodors.com.

TOP REASONS TO GO

■ **Hiking:** Explore the rim trails or journey all the way to the river.

■ **Outdoor adventures:** Rafting, mule riding, biking, and glamping—the Grand Canyon has it all.

■ **Markets:** From weekly farmers' markets to the yearly Indian Market, the city delivers with its local goods.

■ **Skywalk:** Step 70 feet over the rim on this horse-shoe-shaped glass bridge.

■ **Waterfalls:** Five major waterfalls spill down canyon walls, creating swimming holes.

Contents

MAPS

EXPERIENCE GRAND CANYON NATIONAL PARK

12 ULTIMATE EXPERIENCES

Grand Canyon National Park offers terrific experiences that should be on every traveler's list. Here are Fodor's top picks for a memorable trip.

1 Hiking the Trails

One of the park's most popular activities, hiking gives a new perspective on the Grand Canyon, especially if you tackle the trails below the rim. *(Ch. 3, 4, 5)*

2 Biking in the Grand Canyon

Three routes, including a paved Greenway, skirt the South Rim of the Grand Canyon. Pedal your own bike or rent one in the park. *(Ch. 3)*

3 Taking the Train

Live music, storytelling, and a "hold-up" by costumed actors enliven the 65-mile, 2¼-hour journey from Williams to the South Rim aboard the Grand Canyon Railway. *(Ch. 6)*

4 Driving Desert View

Heading east from the entrance at the South Rim, Desert View Drive passes scenic Yaki Point, Tusayan Pueblo, and the Watchtower with its 360-degree, elevated views. *(Ch. 3)*

5 Watching the Sunset

The Grand Canyon is at its dramatic best at the end of the day when yellows, oranges, reds, and purples color its walls. Bring your camera. *(Ch. 3, 4)*

6 Staying in a Historic Lodge

Opened in 1905, El Tovar Hotel is a National Historic Landmark overlooking the South Rim. If you can't get a reservation, treat yourself to lunch in the fine dining room. *(Ch. 3)*

7 Walking the Trail of Time

Designed to explain how the canyon formed and show how long it took, the paved Trail of Time stretches nearly 3 miles with each meter representing one million years. *(Ch. 3)*

8 Stepping over the Edge

The horseshoe-shaped Skywalk at Grand Canyon West extends 70 feet over the rim, offering views through the glass you're standing on to the floor nearly 4,000 feet below. *(Ch. 5)*

9 Riding a Mule to the Bottom

Mule trips are one of the most popular ways to experience the Grand Canyon. Spend half a day in the saddle, or overnight at Phantom Ranch on a multiday trip. *(Ch. 3, 4)*

10 Soaring Overhead

Get a bird's-eye view of the Grand Canyon—and maybe even dip below the rim—on a helicopter ride. Fixed-wing aircraft tours are also available. *(Ch. 3)*

11 Go Rafting on the Colorado River

Rafting down the Colorado River through the Grand Canyon is a classic Arizona experience. Jostle your joints on a day trip or splurge on a multiday adventure. *(Ch. 5, 6)*

12 Exploring Havasu Canyon

Home of the Havasupai people, this offshoot of the Grand Canyon
rewards with towering waterfalls and turquoise pools. Plan to
overnight, as no day hiking is permitted. *(Ch. 5)*

WHAT'S WHERE

1 South Rim. The South Rim is where the action is: Grand Canyon Village's lodging, camping, eateries, stores, and museums, plus plenty of trailheads into the canyon. Four free shuttle routes cover more than 35 stops.

2 North Rim. Most visitors enter the park at the South Rim, but many consider the North Rim even more gorgeous—and worth the extra effort. Open only from mid-May to the end of October (or the first good snowfall), the North Rim has legitimate bragging rights: it's at more than 8,000 feet above sea level (1,000 feet higher than the South Rim).

3 West Rim. Though not in Grand Canyon National Park, the western end of the canyon has some spectacular scenery, especially when viewed from the U-shaped glass-floored Skywalk deck, which juts out 4,000 feet above the Colorado River.

4 Havasu Canyon. See stunning waterfalls in Havasu Canyon, but getting there requires advance reservations.

5 Gateways. Tusayan is a good base for Grand Canyon adventures. Williams, an hour's drive south, offers lodging and dining along historic Route 66, while Flagstaff, an hour and a half away, boasts a university and historic downtown.

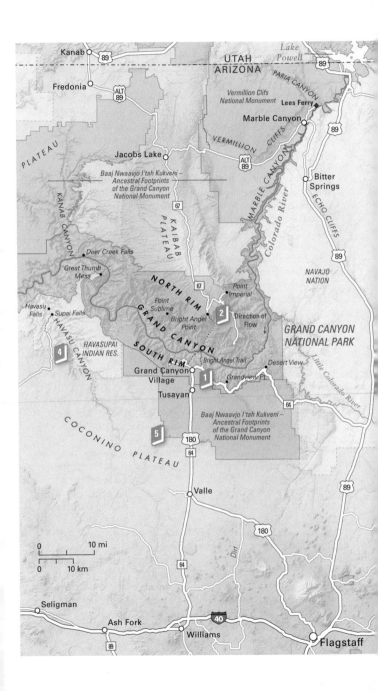

Welcome to the Grand Canyon

The Grand Canyon is far more than an experience, it's an emotion—ask anyone who's visited, hiked, or explored here. Many think it deserves a greater superlative than just "Grand," and although it's easy to list the geographical and historical statistics of the canyon, all that becomes immaterial as you lose your breath when standing at the edge, whether for the first sunrise or the thousandth sunset. The park is more than just the view, though; it offers extraordinary opportunities for adventure, from hiking and biking to riding a mule into its depths and rafting the Colorado River.

GEOLOGICAL WONDERS, INCREDIBLE PROPORTIONS

As you gaze out from the rim, you're viewing two billion years of geologic history, exposed for all to see in the canyon's rock walls. There's more Paleozoic and Pre-Cambrian earth history on display here than anywhere else on the planet. Far below the rim, the Colorado River continues its timeless carving process. It's been estimated that, prior to the completion of the Glen Canyon Dam, an average of 400,000 tons of silt was carried away every day, the equivalent of 80,000 5-ton dump-truck loads—one per second, nonstop.

The Grand Canyon is as vast as its name implies. If you were to travel from one end of the canyon to the other, you would journey just under 280 miles from Lees Ferry near the junction of the Paria and Colorado rivers in northern Arizona to the western border shared by Arizona and Nevada. At its deepest point, the canyon is nearly 6,000 feet. From the North Rim to the South Rim, the distance across varies from 18 miles to less than a ½ mile. However, to travel between rims by car requires a journey of 200 miles.

THE PEOPLE OF THE CANYON

Long before the first Europeans stood on the southern rim of the Grand Canyon—more than 10,000 years ago, to be exact—prehistoric Paleo-Indians wandered through it, followed 8,500 years later by the Ancestral Puebloans. Thought to be ancestors of the Hopi, they built complexes on the rim and farmed on and below it. Some 600 years ago, the Navajo moved into the area. Today, they now live on a large reservation to the east of the national park while the Havasupai and Hualapai live on reservations at the canyon's western end.

The first Europeans to view the canyons were Spanish conquistadors, who were more interested in finding the fabled Seven Cities of Gold than natural wonders, while the first Americans were an army survey party that was also unimpressed. It wasn't until 1869, when John Wesley Powell undertook his famous voyage down the Colorado River, that Americans began to take notice. The first tourists arrived on the Grand Canyon Railway in 1901. Seven years later, the area was declared a national monument, and in 1919, Congress passed legislation making it a national park. Today, more than six million people visit annually.

EARLY INFLUENCES ON THE PARK

Grand Canyon National Park today, particularly the South Rim, owes a lot to the Fred Harvey Company and its chief architect and decorator, Mary Jane Colter. Founded by entrepreneur Fred Harvey, the company established trackside restaurants along the Santa Fe Railroad line. His son, Ford Harvey, continued the tradition, championing the establishment of Grand Canyon National Park and bringing Harvey hospitality here. You can learn more about the Fred Harvey Company through displays at El Tovar Hotel.

While Colter wasn't the architect behind El Tovar, she did design six structures at the Grand Canyon: Hopi House, Hermits Rest, Lookout Studio, Phantom Ranch, Desert View Watchtower, and Bright Angel Lodge. Of the six, Desert View Watchtower, a 70-foot structure modeled after Ancient Puebloan ruins scattered throughout the Southwest, and Hopi House, a multistory structure inspired by the Hopi buildings in Old Oraibi, are the most distinctive, but it's Bright Angel Lodge that may have been most influential. In constructing its famous 10-foot-high fireplace, Colter used canyon rock to mimic the geologic strata found in its walls and shaped it based on the canyon's contours. Subsequently, Bright Angel Lodge became the model for the early architecture in national parks.

Flora of the Grand Canyon

INDIAN PAINTBRUSH
Although it's a bright-red perennial, the Indian paintbrushes' flowers are actually inconspicuous—it's the fire-red bracts beneath each flower that draw the eye.

COLORADO PIÑON
Colorado piñon is the most common pine-tree species found in the widespread juniper woodlands on the Colorado Plateau. Although it can be found on both rims of the Grand Canyon, this popular tree thrives in habitats ranging from 4,000 to 8,000 feet.

WESTERN REDBUD
Clusters of red-purple flowers make this small tree one of the most colorful canyon inhabitants. Look for it along the creek at Havasupai Gardens on the Bright Angel Trail and near seeps and springs in the inner corridors of the Grand Canyon.

CREOSOTE
Abundant in Southwestern deserts, this evergreen shrub bears dark-green, resinous leaves and can be found covering large areas of well-drained flatland. The combination of at least 49 oils gives the plant its characteristic odor.

HILL'S LUPINE
The most common of the nine species of lupine in the park, this dark purplish-blue wildflower blooms from June through August on both rims. You'll find them in Grand Canyon Village, at Yaki Point, on Transept Trail, and in mountain meadows.

PONDEROSA PINE

Ponderosa-pine forests dominate the upper elevations of the far-flung Colorado Plateau, including the Kaibab Forest, where the predominant subspecies is the three-needled Rocky Mountain ponderosa pine.

CATCLAW ACACIA

Also known as Devil's Claw, this Southwestern native with numerous hooked thorns can commonly be found in semidesert grasslands and brushy rangeland in deep arroyos. Catclaw acacia blooms in May, and its fragrant, cream-colored flowers provide fabulous nectar for honey production.

BANANA YUCCA

Named for the large fleshy fruit it produces in summer, this widespread desert plant can be found on both rims but is more predominant on the drier South Rim.

ENGELMANN SPRUCE

Found in the upper reaches of the Kaibab Plateau, the Engelmann spruce is one of the tallest trees on the North Rim. This hardy tree lives up to 600 years and stands up to 160 feet tall with a trunk of about 40 inches.

UTAH JUNIPER

This small, gnarled evergreen rarely grows taller than 15 feet and is recognizable by its spiny, branched fronds; bluish-gray berries; and easily shredded, grayish-brown bark.

Fauna of the Grand Canyon

MULE DEER
One of the most commonly seen animals in Grand Canyon National Park, these deer are named for their trademark large ears. They can easily adapt to a variety of habitats within the park, from forests to the desert and riparian areas along the Colorado River.

BISON
Descendants of bison that migrated to the area in the early 1990s, the House Rock herd graze inside the canyon's North Rim boundary and in the surrounding forest.

CANYON BAT
Formerly known as the western pipistrelle, this is the smallest bat in North America, weighing a mere 3 to 6 grams, just slightly more than a penny. It is usually the first bat out at night and roosts in narrow rocky cliffside crevices.

MOUNTAIN LION
Since they're nocturnal, you probably won't see a mountain lion in the park, but these carnivores hunt mule deer and elk. Drive carefully after dark to avoid hitting them, and don't worry about becoming dinner—they don't see humans as prey.

CALIFORNIA CONDOR
Once nearly extinct, these opportunistic scavengers soar through the Grand Canyon today thanks to a conservation project. With their 10-foot wingspans and bald, pinkish-orange heads, they're easy to spot at the South Rim.

GILA MONSTER

This large, venomous lizard is native to the Southwest and can be identified by its patterned orange and black scales. Although their venom is usually not fatal, the bite can be very painful.

COYOTE

Coyotes thrive throughout the Southwest in a variety of habitats, including the Grand Canyon. More often heard than seen, they exercise a diverse vocal repertoire filled with barks, wails, and yips.

DESERT BIGHORN SHEEP

The largest native animal in the canyon, desert bighorn sheep are known for their rugged aggressiveness, tenacious footwork, and ability to survive inhospitable landscapes.

KAIBAB SQUIRREL

Related to the Abert's squirrel you'll see at the South Rim, this brownish-black, tassel-eared squirrel with a bushy white tail has evolved into its own subspecies. It lives exclusively in the ponderosa-pine forests on the Kaibab Plateau and feeds on ponderosa-pine seeds, bark, and twigs.

GRAND CANYON RATTLESNAKE

Of the six species of rattlesnakes found in the park, the venomous Grand Canyon pink rattlesnake is the most common. It typically hibernates in the winter and is most often seen early mornings and late afternoons in the spring and fall.

Best Hikes of the Grand Canyon

HAVASU FALLS

It's a 10-mile hike from Hualapai Hilltop on the Havasupai Reservation to the campground below, but you can spend the next several days exploring Havasu Canyon's five major waterfalls.

NORTH KAIBAB TRAIL

The only maintained route into the canyon from the North Rim, this trail ends at Bright Angel Campground, but only the physically fit should attempt to go farther than Roaring Springs, a strenuous 3,050 feet below the rim.

BRIGHT ANGEL POINT TRAIL

The busiest trail on the North Rim, this easy, ½-mile walk begins near the visitor center and ends at the panoramic overlook of Bright Angel Canyon. Take your time—the elevation here is more than 7,000 feet—and enjoy the view.

GRANDVIEW TRAIL

Originally a mining route, Grandview Trail is one of the most rugged and remote trails in the Grand Canyon. Take it 3 miles to Horseshoe Mesa, 3½-plus miles to Page Springs, or 4½ miles to Cottonwood Creek.

HERMIT TRAIL

Just past Hermits Rest on the South Rim, this rocky trail drops for the first 2½ miles, then continues another mile to Dripping Springs, a shaded alcove spring in Hermit Canyon. Plan to be on the trail for at least five hours round-trip.

South Kaibab Trail

SOUTH KAIBAB TRAIL

Another good trail for day hikers, this steep South Rim trail has three turnaround points: the unmarked Ooh-Aah Point 1 mile from the rim, Cedar Ridge at 1½ miles, and Skeleton Point 3 miles down. Stop at Cedar Ridge during the summer.

ARIZONA TRAIL

Divided into 43 passages, this epic trail runs through the state from Mexico to Utah. To hike it through the Grand Canyon, start at the Grandview Lookout Tower, hike the South and North Kaibab trails through the canyon, and end at Kaibab National Forest.

KEN PATRICK TRAIL

Skirting the North Rim from Point Imperial to the North Kaibab Trail parking lot, this moderately challenging, 10-mile hike passes through ponderosa pines and alpine meadows and is at its best in June when wildflowers bloom.

RIM TRAIL

This partially paved, relatively flat trail stretches 13 miles along the South Rim from Grand Canyon Village to Hermits Rest. Shuttle stops at Monument Creek Vista, Pima Point, and Hermits Rest make it easy to customize just how far you go.

The Grand Canyon with Kids

From hiking and rafting in the national park to stepping across the glass Skywalk at the West Rim, the Grand Canyon is full of outdoor adventure for family members of all ages. Plan to stay over at least one night on the rim or in the canyon, so you can explore unrushed.

HIKING

Many Grand Canyon hikes are extremely challenging, but a number are suitable for all ages. One of the best for families is the Rim Trail, which stretches 13 miles from the South Kaibab Trailhead to Hermits Rest. Shuttle stops along the way make it easy to end the hike whenever you're ready to turn back, and geology exhibits from Yavapai Point to Verkamp's Visitor Center keep kids engaged along the way. Older kids can manage a day hike a short distance below the rim or to the bottom (but only if you plan to spend at least one day recuperating before heading back up).

BICYCLING

Kids will have a blast pedaling from one overlook to another along the South Rim on their own bicycle or one rented from Bright Angel Bicycles, the park's only authorized concessioner. Not only does Bright Angel Bicycles rent cruiser-style bicycles for adults and children, it also rents Burley trailers to tow tots and tag-alongs for beginner bikers, so the whole family can explore the rim from Yaki Point to Hermits Rest. Pick up sandwiches from Bright Angel Bicycles' café before heading out and have a picnic along the way.

MULE RIDE

Hiking isn't the only way to get to the bottom of the canyon. Families with children nine and up (and at least 4 feet 9 inches tall) can ride sure-footed mules down the Bright Angel Trail to Phantom Ranch and stay one night or two before saddling up for a return. Afraid of heights? Choose the rim-level Canyon Vista ride instead. Advance reservations are required, especially in the summer; sometimes there is walk-up availability in the winter. You can ride at both the North and South rims.

RAFTING THE RIVER

Families can brave the rapids on one-day or multiday rafting trips on either the east or west end of the Grand Canyon. Depending on how much effort you want to exert, opt for a motorized raft (the most comfortable), oar boat, or a hybrid. Most rafting trips require participants to be at least seven years old and willing to camp in tents on shore overnight. Since these trips tend to sell out, you'll want to make reservations well in advance, especially if you plan to visit during the peak summer months.

TAKING THE TRAIN

Getting to the Grand Canyon's South Rim can be just as much of an adventure as visiting the canyon itself if you go by train. The Grand Canyon Railway's restored locomotives and vintage cars depart Williams every morning following a shootout at the depot between the Marshall and the Cataract Creek Gang. During the two-hour journey to the rim, costumed storytellers, singers, and train robbers entertain passengers. You can return on the train later that afternoon, but many families prefer to overnight at Maswik Lodge, so they can spend more time at the canyon.

STARRY NIGHTS

Grand Canyon National Park is an International Dark Sky Park, meaning it not only is committed to minimizing light pollution but also hosts astronomy-related ranger programs. Every June, the North and South rims host a Star Party with family-friendly lectures, activities, and telescope viewing. Like the ranger programs, the Star Party is free with admission.

JUNIOR RANGER PROGRAMS

Grand Canyon National Park offers three junior ranger programs: South Rim for ages four and up, North Rim for ages five and up, and Grand Canyon Junior Explorer Rangers for all ages who visit the bottom of the canyon or Tuweep. Pick up a South Rim Junior Ranger Activity Book at the Grand Canyon Conservancy Main Store, Yavapai Geology Museum, or Kolb Studio; a North Rim activity book at the North Rim Visitor Center; or an Explorer Ranger activity book at trail campgrounds or backcountry ranger stations.

GRAND CANYON CONSERVANCY FIELD INSTITUTE

A nonprofit partner of Grand Canyon National Park, the Grand Canyon Conservancy Field Institute offers a mix of family-friendly classes, guided hiking trips, and educational tours led by geologists, historians, ecologists, archaeologists, and other experts. The programs can be a splurge, but it's worth it for families fascinated by a particular topic, like wildlife in the canyon, or who share a common interest, like photography.

What to Watch and Read

OVER THE EDGE: DEATH IN THE GRAND CANYON

This book by coauthors Michael P. Ghiglieri and Thomas M. Myers tells the stories behind 550 of the approximately 800 deaths that have occurred at the Grand Canyon since 1869.

I AM THE GRAND CANYON: THE STORY OF THE HAVASUPAI PEOPLE

Author Stephen Hirst details the Havasupai tribe's fight to reclaim their traditional lands in the Grand Canyon and on the Colorado Plateau from the federal government. Today, after a return of thousands of acres, the Havasupai offer rafting trips through their lands and manage the West Rim.

SKELETON MAN

Navajo Tribal Police Lieutenant Joe Leaphorn and Sergeant Jim Chee search the Grand Canyon for a skeleton handcuffed to a fortune of diamonds as they try to solve a trading post robbery in this Tony Hillerman bestseller. A 1956 midair collision over the canyon plays a part in the plot.

THE EXPLORATION OF THE COLORADO RIVER AND ITS CANYONS

Explorer and geologist John Wesley Powell gives a first-person account of his 1869 expedition down the Green and Colorado rivers and through the Grand Canyon.

LAST OF THE GREAT UNKNOWN

This 2012 documentary follows a team of canyoneers as they explore some of the hundreds of slot canyons in the Grand Canyon. If you can't hike into the canyon, it's a good look at what's below the rim.

LONG ROAD TO MERCY

David Baldacci introduces FBI agent Atlee Pine in this novel involving the murder of a Grand Canyon mule. As Pine searches for its missing rider, she realizes the case is much bigger than she thought—democracy is at stake.

INTO THE CANYON

Filmmaker Pete McBride and writer Kevin Fedarko attempt to hike the entire 750-mile length of the Grand Canyon in this 2019 documentary. Not only do they face physical challenges along the way but they note threats to the canyon itself, including tourism and possible uranium drilling.

THE WEIGHT OF WATER

Blind kayaker Erik Weihenmayer faces his fears and the rapids as he navigates the length of the Grand Canyon in this 2018 documentary.

TRAVEL SMART

Updated by
Teresa Bitler

★ **CAPITAL:**
Phoenix

♱ **POPULATION:**
7,151,502 (AZ)

💬 **LANGUAGE:**
English

$ **CURRENCY:**
U.S. dollar

☏ **AREA CODES:**
480, 520, 602, 623, 928

⚠ **EMERGENCIES:**
911

🚗 **DRIVING:**
On the right

⚡ **ELECTRICITY:**
120–220 v/60 cycles;
plugs have two or
three rectangular
prongs

🕙 **TIME:**
In the summer, three
hours behind New
York; in the winter, two
hours behind New York

🌐 **WEB RESOURCES:**
www.nps.gov/grca
www.visitarizona.com
www.flagstaffarizona.
org

✈ **AIRPORTS:**
PHX, FLG, GCN

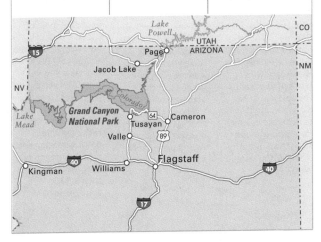

Know Before You Go

Stretching 277 river miles, with an average width of 10 miles across and a depth of 1 mile, the Grand Canyon is a superstar—biologically, historically, and recreationally. More than six million people visit the park every year to appreciate its grandeur and to hike, bike, raft, camp, and more. Here are a few tips and recommendations to ensure you enjoy all the Grand Canyon has to offer and to keep you safe while you're visiting.

KNOW THE LAYOUT

Grand Canyon National Park is divided into two sections: the North Rim and the South Rim. Although they are only 10 miles apart rim to rim, getting from one to the other is a 210-mile, nearly four-hour drive. Similarly, the West Rim—Grand Canyon West and Havasu Canyon—is not part of the national park; it is on Hualapai and Havasupai tribal lands. If you want to experience the Skywalk, you'll have to drive 240 miles (four hours) to get from the South Rim to Grand Canyon West.

RESPECT NATIVE LANDS

You may find yourself on Native American lands. Grand Canyon West is managed by the Hualapai tribe, Havasu Canyon is the home of the Havasupai people, and the Navajo Nation sits east of the canyon. Alcohol is strictly prohibited on tribal lands; just consuming alcohol can lead to jail time. Drugs, weapons, nudity, and drones also are prohibited. When you visit, dress conservatively, and don't photograph a tribe member without asking permission first.

PLAN 13 MONTHS AHEAD

Sure, you can visit on a whim if you're content to see the canyon on a day trip. However, if you want to overnight inside the park, you'll need to book when reservations open, usually 13 months in advance. Same goes with rafting trips, mule rides, and permits to hike into Havasu Canyon. If you want to stay in Tusayan, especially in the summer, reserve your room at least six months ahead of your stay. Book air tours, jeep tours, and other activities well in advance, too.

STAY BACK

It seems to go without saying that where there isn't a railing—and that applies to most of the North, South, and West Rims—you should stay back from the canyon's edge. And yet, every year, several people fall to their deaths. Most frequently, these accidents occur when someone is pretending to fall over (and then loses their balance and actually does) or posing for a picture and doesn't realize how close to the edge they are. Use extreme caution anytime you are near the edge, and don't lose sight of your children.

DAY HIKES
There are several day hikes at both the North Rim and the South Rim; hiking to the canyon floor and back isn't one of them. The National Park Service strongly discourages hikers, no matter how experienced or physically fit, from attempting such a feat, especially from May to September when temperatures soar to triple digits inside the canyon. Instead, plan one day to hike into the canyon, at least one day in the canyon, and then another day to hike back out.

TRAIL ETIQUETTE
When hiking Grand Canyon trails, follow basic Leave No Trace principles: know your route, stay on main trails, pack out what you bring in, leave what you find (in particular artifacts and archaeological

remains), and keep your voice at a reasonable level. But the Grand Canyon builds on those. On canyon trails, mules and uphill hikers have the right of way. If you want to pass, let the people ahead know your intentions. (Keep in mind some people don't speak English.) Finally, fires are not permitted below the rim.

GET PERMITTED
If you plan to camp below the rim on a multiday hike, you'll need a backcountry permit. Permits are $10 plus $12 per person or stock animal per night. Hikers who want to overnight at Phantom Ranch or adjoining campground at the bottom of the Grand Canyon must secure a reservation through a lottery system. To hike into Havasu Canyon, you'll also need a permit obtained through lottery from the Havasupai tribe; you'll be stopped at several points on the trail and asked to show your permit.

Getting Here and Around

Air

Although there are regional airports closer to the Grand Canyon, most visitors who arrive by air fly into one of the major airports and make the last leg of the trip by car. The closest major airport to the South Rim is Phoenix Sky Harbor International Airport (PHX), about 250 miles south of the park's southern entrance and 426 miles southwest of its eastern entrance. If you plan to visit the North Rim or West Rim, Harry Reid International Airport (LAS) in Las Vegas is the closest option. Harry Reid International Airport is 265 miles east of the North Rim and 125 miles northwest of Grand Canyon West on the West Rim. There are some direct flights from Salt Lake City and Denver into St. George Regional Airport (SGU), just 150 miles northwest of the North Rim, and a few daily flights from Phoenix and Dallas to Flagstaff Pulliam Airport (FLG), about 100 miles southeast of the South Rim.

AIRPORTS

The national park has its own airport, Grand Canyon National Airport (GCN) on the southern edge of Tusayan, just minutes from the park's southern entrance. While there are some direct flights from Las Vegas, primarily this airport is used by helicopters to take passengers on tours of the canyon. The North Rim does not have an airport.

Similarly, there is a small airport at the West Rim, Grand Canyon West Airport (GCW). Although a few chartered flights from Las Vegas land here, it is also used mainly by companies offering helicopter tours of the canyon's western edge.

Car

Most of Arizona's scenic highlights are many miles apart, and a car is essential for touring the state. However, you technically don't need one if you're planning to visit only the Grand Canyon's most popular area, the South Rim. You can fly to Flagstaff and take a shuttle or taxi to the Grand Canyon, fly directly from Las Vegas to the Grand Canyon, or take a shuttle from Phoenix. If you are visiting Las Vegas, you can take a shuttle, bus, or 4x4 tour to the West Rim.

If you're driving to Arizona from the east or coming up from the southern part of the state, the best access to the Grand Canyon is from Flagstaff. You can take U.S. 180 northwest 80 miles to Grand Canyon Village on the South Rim. Or, for a scenic route with stopping points along the canyon rim, drive north on U.S. 89 from Flagstaff, turn left at the junction of Highway 64 (52 miles north of Flagstaff), which merges with U.S. 180 at Valle (Grand Canyon Junction), and proceed north and west for an additional 57 miles until you reach Grand Canyon Village on the South Rim.

If you're crossing Arizona on U.S. 40 from the west, your most direct route to the South Rim is on Highway 64 (U.S. 180), which runs north from Williams 58 miles to Grand Canyon Village. For road and weather conditions, call ☎ 511 in Arizona or ☎ 888/411–7623 out of state, or visit ⊕ az511.com.

If you're driving to Grand Canyon West from Kingman, take the Stockton Hill Road exit off Interstate 40. Head north to Pierce Ferry Road. Travel north for 7 miles to Diamond Bar Road and turn east. In 21 miles, Diamond Bar Road comes to a dead end at Grand Canyon West Airport. From Las Vegas, take U.S. 95/U.S. 93 south (29 miles) to Pierce Ferry Road. Turn left (east). Continue 29 miles to Diamond Bar Road. Turn right and drive for 21 miles until Diamond Bar Road dead-ends at the airport and Grand Canyon West.

CAR RENTALS

If you're arriving by air, it usually makes sense to rent a car because of the distances involved in getting to the Grand Canyon and around this part of the Southwest. Visitors flying into Phoenix Sky Harbor International Airport can rent one of up to 5,600 cars available at its Rental Car Center, which can easily be reached by shuttle on the baggage claim levels of each terminal. Note that you will pay slightly more for the convenience of renting a car at the airport versus taking a rideshare to an offsite rental facility. Rental car prices are very seasonal in Phoenix. High season is January through March, when events like the Waste Management Phoenix Open, Cactus League Spring Training, and occasional Super Bowl drive up demand. In summer, rates are substantially lower.

Although you don't need a rental car to visit Grand Canyon West from Las Vegas, if you want to explore more of the Southwest or visit the North Rim or South Rim, you will want to rent one at Harry Reid International Airport. Just take the free shuttle to the airport's Rent-A-Car Center, where you can choose from the available models offered by 11 car rental companies. Like Phoenix, the low season in Las Vegas is

Getting Here and Around

July through August; rental car prices are cheapest then.

It's also possible to rent a car if you fly into a regional airport, such as Flagstaff Pulliam Airport or St. George Regional Airport. However, expect to pay $10 more per day on average for a car rental at these smaller airports than you would at the international airports, where there's more selection as well.

GASOLINE

The only gas station inside the national park on the South Rim is at Desert View, and this station operates only from March 31 to September 30 depending on snowfall. There is no gas station in Grand Canyon Village. Gas and diesel are available year-round at the South Entrance in Tusayan and at Cameron, to the east.

At the South Rim, in Grand Canyon Village, the Public Garage is a fully equipped AAA garage that provides auto repair daily 8 am to noon and 1 to 5 pm, as well as 24-hour emergency service. This a garage for simple repairs such as tires, belts, batteries, fuses, and hoses; more difficult repairs are towed to Williams or Flagstaff. No gas is available at the Public Garage.

At the North Rim, the Chevron service station, which repairs autos, is inside the park on the access road leading to the North Rim Campground. The station is open daily 8 to 5, mid-May through mid-October, and sells pay-at-the-pump gasoline and diesel fuel 24 hours a day.

On the way to Grand Canyon West, fuel can be purchased at the gas station on the corner or Pierce Ferry Road and U.S. 93 or before leaving Dolan Springs, also on Pierce Ferry Road. In a pinch, you can purchase gas at Grand Canyon West; inquire about availability at one of the gift shops. If you are taking Route 66 to Hualapai Hilltop to hike into Havasu Canyon, you can purchase gas in Seligman and Kingman at either end of the Mother Road or at the gas station across the street from Hualapai Lodge in Peach Springs. There is no gas at Hualapai Hilltop.

PARKING

Approaching Grand Canyon Village on the South Rim from the Southern Entrance, your first opportunity to park is in one of the four lots surrounding Grand Canyon Visitor Plaza. (Lot 1 is the only one with designated RV parking.) The park strongly encourages—and at times, during the summer, requires—visitors to park here and take the shuttle to the western viewpoints and Grand Canyon Village. The RV parking spots sometimes fill up during the summer, spring break, and holidays; at those times, those traveling with RVs may be directed to additional RV parking at the Shrine of Ages, Yavapai Lodge, or the Backcountry Information Center.

Beyond the visitor center lots, parking is limited to the lot at Grand Canyon Village as you head west. However, parking in Grand Canyon Village is always difficult and, during high season, may be reserved for guests staying at the hotel or the lodges. Going east on Desert View Drive, every overlook except Yaki Point has parking available.

At the North Rim, there is parking at the North Rim Visitor Center near Grand Canyon Lodge, at the general store near the campground, at the North Kaibab Trailhead, and at the Cape Royal Trailhead.

Parking isn't an issue at Grand Canyon West; all visitors must park and ride the shuttle to the facilities and overlooks there. At Hualapai Hilltop, hikers are required to park before heading into Havasu Canyon. The parking lot there is monitored.

ROAD CONDITIONS

When driving off major highways in low-lying areas, watch for rain clouds. Flash floods from sudden summer rains can be deadly.

The South Rim stays open to auto traffic year-round, although access to Hermits Rest is limited to shuttle buses in summer because of congestion. Roads leading to the South Rim near Grand Canyon Village and the parking areas along the rim are congested in summer as well. If you visit from October through April, you can experience only light to moderate traffic and have no problem with parking.

Reaching elevations of 8,000 feet, the more remote North Rim has no services available from late October through mid-May. Highway 67 south of Jacob Lake is closed by the first heavy snowfall in November or December and remains closed until early to mid-May.

At one point, the Diamond Bar Road heading to Grand Canyon West was a teeth-jarring experience, but it is now paved. Watch for cattle as you make the drive; cars coming and going from Grand Canyon West collide with cattle roaming the desert here as frequently as once a week.

Getting Here and Around

To check on Arizona road conditions, dial ☎ *511* from anywhere within the state or ☎ *888/411–7623* outside the state. You can also visit ⊕ *az511.com* for online information.

ROADSIDE EMERGENCIES

In the event of a roadside emergency, call ☎ *911*. Depending on the location, either the state police or the county sheriff's department will respond. Call the city or village police department if you encounter trouble within the limits of a municipality. Indian reservations have tribal police headquarters, and rangers assist travelers within the U.S. Forest Service boundaries.

Ride-Sharing

Rideshare companies operate in the communities near the South Rim but may be limited due to the number of drivers available at any given time and the amount of money they can make driving to the South Rim. You can hire a rideshare to take you to the Grand Canyon, if available, from Flagstaff (approximately $175), Williams (approximately $140), or Tusayan (approximately $60). If you want to go from Las Vegas to Grand Canyon West, you can get a rideshare

for approximately $150; it will cost approximately $220 to get from Las Vegas to the South Rim, if you can find a driver willing to take you. Hualapai Hilltop and the North Rim are so remote that rideshares are not a practical option.

Taxi

Visitors to the South Rim can catch a cab from the Grand Canyon Airport and hotels in Tusayan by calling the taxi service operated by Xanterra (☎ *928/638–2631*). Williams Taxi and Shuttle (☎ *928/635–1111* ⊕ *www.williamstaxi.com*) takes travelers to the South Rim from Williams.

🚆 Train

Amtrak offers train service from stations nationwide to Flagstaff and Williams. To ride the rails direct to the South Rim in Grand Canyon National Park, hop aboard the cozy cars on the Grand Canyon Railway, which has been taking spectators to the Grand Canyon since 1901.

Essentials

Admission Fees

Admission fees for Grand Canyon National Park are $35 per vehicle; $30 per motorcycle; and $20 per bicyclist, hiker, or pedestrian. Admission is valid for seven days and good for both rims. The fees are collected at the south entrance near Tusayan and at the east entrance near Cameron for the South Rim and at the main entrance at the North Rim. The Grand Canyon pass, available for $70, gives unlimited access to the park for 12 months from the purchase date. The America the Beautiful Pass, available for $80, gives unlimited access to all federal recreation areas and national parks for 12 months. The America the Beautiful Senior Pass has the same benefits for U.S. citizens age 62 or older for the cost of $20 annually or $80 for life; the military version grants active duty military personnel and dependents free admission.

Outside the national park, you will have to pay to visit Grand Canyon West and Havasu Canyon. Entrance fees to the tribal lands at each location are included in ticket prices and permits. General admission to Grand Canyon West, including Eagle Point and Guano Point, is $49; a package including the Skywalk is $64. Permits to Havasu Falls cost $100

(weekday) or $125 (weekend) per person per night with a three-night minimum stay required and include all taxes and environmental fees.

Dining

PAYING

Most restaurants take credit cards, but some smaller places do not, so it's worth asking.

⇨ *Prices in the restaurant reviews are the average cost of a main course at dinner or, if dinner is not served, at lunch.*

What It Costs in U.S. Dollars			
$	$$	$$$	$$$$
AT DINNER			
under $12	$12–$20	$21–$30	over $30

RESERVATIONS AND DRESS

Dress is never formal in a national park, but you may want to put on your best jeans (or even slacks) if you intend to dine at the El Tovar Dining Room, the fanciest place at the South Rim, or at the Main Lodge Dining Room at Grand Canyon Lodge on the North Rim. Reservations are a necessity at El Tovar.

Outside the park, dress is usually casual as well, especially in the smaller communities. A few high-end restaurants in

Essentials

Flagstaff require reservations, and you may fit in better at these places wearing, at the very least, clean jeans without holes and a nice shirt.

MEALS AND MEALTIMES
In the national park, most restaurants serving breakfast open at 7 am and those serving dinner remain open until 9 pm. Some coffeehouses open as early as 5 am, though, and some bars turn off the lights closer to midnight.

Sky View Restaurant, the main dining option at Grand Canyon West, is open 9 am to 4:15 pm. In Havasu Canyon, although there is a café in Supai, you are mainly responsible for bringing and preparing your own meals.

SMOKING
Smoking is prohibited in national parks. This includes smoking tobacco or cannabis as well as vaping. Local ordinances apply outside the national park.

🛏 Lodging

FACILITIES
You can assume that all rooms have private baths, phones, internet, TVs, and air-conditioning, unless otherwise indicated. (In general, though, air-conditioning and internet are a luxury at the more remote motels and lodges on the way to the North Rim.) Breakfast is not a typical perk unless you're staying at a name-brand hotel in Flagstaff, Williams, or Tusayan, or you're staying at a bed-and-breakfast. There are a few hotels with pools, though some are indoors.

PARKING
Parking is typically included with your stay at national park lodges and in the gateway communities.

PRICES
Rates are fairly static in the park and in nearby communities. If you're arriving in Phoenix or Las Vegas before making your way to the Grand Canyon, rates drop by 50% or more Memorial Day through Labor Day, and peak in the winter.

⇨ *Prices are the average cost of a double room during high season, not including especially expensive holiday or special-event rates.*

What It Costs in U.S. Dollars			
$	$$	$$$	$$$$
LODGING FOR TWO			
under $120	$120–$175	$176–$250	over $250

RESERVATIONS
You will need to make a reservation up to 13 months in advance if you want to stay

inside Grand Canyon National Park. A stay in Tusayan requires making reservations six months or more in advance, especially during the summer, at spring break, or during the holidays. Flagstaff and Williams don't require reservations quite so far in advance but should be booked before you go.

🗂 Packing

Temperatures at night and in the morning can be quite chilly, even during the summer, and much warmer during the day. Temperatures inside the canyon can be 20°F hotter than at the rim; on a summer day, it can be 60°F on the South Rim when you start hiking and over 100°F by the time you get to the bottom of the canyon. Pack so that you can dress in layers.

Always pack sturdy, close-toed shoes, a hat, sunglasses, and plenty of sunscreen.

💲 Taxes

Arizona state sales tax (called a transaction privilege tax), which applies to all purchases except food in grocery stores, is 5.6%. In Flagstaff, you will pay 9.18%, which includes the state tax plus county and city taxes. Some restaurants in

Flagstaff are also charging an additional percentage to offset the city's recent adoption of a $16.80 per hour minimum wage ($14.80 for tipped hourly workers). Total sales taxes throughout the state range from 7.3% to 10.7%. Sales taxes do not apply on Native American reservations.

💵 Tipping

Tipping is expected at sit-down restaurants and bars, with some restaurants automatically adding a 20% gratuity on parties of six or more. Generally, diners tip 20% for average service and 25% for exceptional service. At coffeehouses, leaving a few dollars in the tip jar is the norm.

At a hotel or resort, tip the bellboy $5–$10 for bringing your luggage to the room (or to the lobby when you leave), a similar amount for housekeeping every day, and $5 for the valet who brings your car.

On a tour, it is common to tip the guide. Usually, this will be 20%, although some tour companies post guidelines to indicate how much is considered an appropriate amount for the guide's services. If uncertain how much to tip your guide, ask when booking your tour.

Essentials

Tipping Guide for Arizona

Bartender	$1–$5 per round of drinks, depending on the number of drinks
Bellhop	$1–$5 per bag, depending on the level of the hotel
Coat check	$1–$2 per coat
Hotel concierge	$5 or more, depending on the service
Hotel doorstaff	$1–$5 for help with bags or hailing a cab
Hotel maid	$2–$5 a day (in cash, preferably daily since cleaning staff may be different each day you stay)
Hotel room service waiter	$1–$2 per delivery, even if a service charge has been added
Porter at airport or train station	$1 per bag
Restroom attendants	$1 or small change
Skycap at airport	$1–$3 per bag checked
Spa personnel	15%–20% of the cost of your service
Taxi driver	15%–20%
Tour guide	10%–15% of the cost of the tour, per person
Valet parking attendant	$2–$5, each time your car is brought to you
Waiter	15%–20%, with 20% being the norm at high-end restaurants; nothing additional if a service charge is added to the bill

◉ Visitor Information

There are two visitor centers at the South Rim (the Grand Canyon Visitor Center and Verkamp's Visitor Center), and one at the North Rim. Everyone arriving at the National Park is given a detailed map of the area; a free newspaper, *The Guide*, is available at visitor centers. The park also distributes a free Accessibility Guide for travelers with disabilities.

📅 When to Go

Low season: Winter is the quietest time on the South Rim. Two of the main shuttle lines suspend operation, several restaurants close for the season, and activities are curtailed. However, it can be one of the most magical times to experience the canyon, when snow often covers its formations. If you don't mind the cold, it's a great time to visit as long as you don't intend to hike into the canyon; the trails can get icy. The North Rim is closed October 15 through May 15, due to heavy snows that force Highway 67 leading into the park to close. The West Rim of the Grand Canyon, including Havasu Canyon, is open year-round. However, the pools in the canyon are too cold for most people to swim December through February.

Shoulder season: Spring (with the exception of spring break) and fall are the best times to visit. At the South Rim, the days are typically sunny, although there is an occasional snowstorm through March. Closed shuttle routes, restaurants, and activities begin to reopen starting in March. March and April can also be the best time to visit Havasu Canyon; as the snow begins to melt, the waterfalls experience increased flow, and although the pools will still be chilly, the water should be swimmable. Fall is an especially good time to visit the North Rim because the leaves on the aspen trees change color, usually in early October. (If fall color arrives later in October, you can still typically drive Highway 67 until the first major snowstorm sometime in November; the park just won't be open.)

High season: The biggest crowds arrive during the summer (as well as spring break and holidays). Beat the crowds at the South Rim by coming on weekdays or early in the day, before 10 am. The North Rim is an even better option for those looking to avoid crowds, since it receives only 10% of the park's total visitors and is on average 10°F cooler. On the West Rim, summer vacationers come in steady streams from Las Vegas; since there are few trees, prepare for direct beating sunlight. From mid-July to September, monsoon storms roll across the canyon at all three rims. Often these days begin clear and sunny, only to have clouds gather and burst with torrential rains by afternoon. The rain is usually short lived and often thins the crowd for the rest of the day.

Great Itineraries

The Best of the Grand Canyon in 7 Days

Most visitors to Grand Canyon National Park spend their time at the South Rim. Staying overnight in the park or in Tusayan at the South Entrance maximizes the time you can explore everything the canyon has to offer at the South Rim. Plan to spend at least two full days in the park regardless of whether you stay at the North Rim or South Rim. Grand Canyon West is best explored in one day, and Havasu Canyon requires visitors to overnight at least three nights, allowing ample time to hike to the waterfalls.

DAY 1

Start early and drive to the South Rim's **Grand Canyon Visitor Center,** just north of the South Entrance, to pick up info and see your first incredible view at **Mather Point**. Walk the **Rim Trail** a little more than a ½ mile to **Yavapai Point and Geology Museum**, then take the shuttle to **Grand Canyon Village** or continue another 1½ miles by foot on **The Trail of Time**. After lunch in the village, step inside the historic **El Tovar Hotel**, shop for souvenirs at **Hopi House**, and visit **Lookout Studio** and **Kolb Studio**. Board the shuttle heading to **Hermits Rest** and stop at **Hopi Point** on the way back to the visitor center and watch the sunset.

DAY 2

Grab a picnic lunch and, after entering the park, head east on **Desert View Drive**, stopping first at **Yaki Point**. From there, continue driving 7 miles east to **Grandview Point** for a good look of the buttes Krishna Shrine and Vishnu Temple. Go 4 miles east and catch the view at **Moran Point**. Continue to **Lipan Point**, **Navajo Point**, and **Desert View and Watchtower**. Stop at one of the picnic areas along the way for lunch. In the afternoon, rent bikes, take a 4x4 tour, or fly over the canyon for a bird's-eye view.

DAY 3

Get an early start and hike part of the way into the canyon via the **Bright Angel Trail**. The first switchback nearly half a mile into the canyon and the 1.5 Mile Resthouse are popular turnarounds. Do not hike farther than Havasupai Gardens, 4½ miles into the canyon (9 miles roundtrip), on a day hike, especially in summer. If you're lucky enough to have reservations for a mule ride, the third day would be a good day for it. Or, spend the day in a program hosted by the **Grand Canyon Conservancy Field Institute**.

DAY 4

Leave the South Rim for the North Rim. **Cameron Trading Post** makes a good place to stretch your legs while shopping for authentic Native American crafts. Veer west on U.S. 89A and stop at **Navajo Bridge** for a glimpse of the Colorado River below. Consider a seven-mile detour to **Lees Ferry** to watch rafters float by, then lunch at one of the motel restaurants near the **Vermillion Cliffs** before heading to higher elevations. Arrive at the North Rim just in time to watch the sunset from the patio of **Grand Canyon Lodge**.

DAY 5

Start the day with a short but sometimes steep hike from the lodge to **Bright Angel Point** for a classic North Rim view, then pack a picnic lunch and drive Cape Royal Road. Stop at **Point Imperial**, **Vista Encantada**, and **Roosevelt Point**. Break up the rim views with a stop at **Walhalla Glades Pueblo**, then continue to **Walhalla Overlook**. Picnic at **Cape Royal** before hiking to **Angels Window** and Cape Royal. At the visitor center, check the schedule for ranger programs to round out your day.

DAY 6

Lace up your hiking boots and hit the trails. The North Rim offers a good variety of easy to challenging hikes. **Transept Trail** is an easy, 4-mile trek (round-trip) that ends with views of a breathtaking side canyon while the **Uncle Jim Trail** meanders through a forest to a viewpoint overlooking the **North Kaibab Trail** into the canyon. The one-way, nearly 10-mile **Ken Patrick Trail** stretches from Point Imperial to the North Kaibab Trail parking lot. As an alternative to hiking, plan a one- or three-hour mule trip for your second day.

DAY 7

Enjoy the sunrise from the patio at Grand Canyon Lodge or **Cape Royal** before heading back toward Cameron. Sample fry bread at **Cameron Trading Post** and arrive in Flagstaff that afternoon. If you have time, shop in the historic downtown or learn more about the Colorado Plateau at the **Museum of Northern Arizona**. After dark, head to **Lowell Observatory**, where Pluto was discovered in 1930, and gaze up at the stars.

On the Calendar

January

Desert View Cultural Demonstrator Series. Grand Canyon National Park hosts dancers, weavers, potters, sculptors, silversmiths, and other artisans at the Grand Canyon Visitor Center and the plaza at Desert View Watchtower throughout the year. Demonstrations are free. ⊕ *www.nps.gov/grca.*

February

I Heart Pluto Festival. This multiday festival of free events celebrates Pluto's discovery at Lowell Observatory in Flagstaff with lectures, tours, and more. ⊕ *iheartpluto.org.*

Arizona Beer Week. The Flagstaff Brewery Trail celebrates the state's sudsy creations with tastings, tap takeovers, beer dinners, and more. ⊕ *craftbeer-flg.com.*

March

Steam Saturdays. Every first Saturday from March through October, vintage steam engines pull the Grand Canyon Railway into Grand Canyon National Park. ⊕ *www.thetrain.com/events/steam-saturdays.*

April

Kite Day. Take advantage of northern Arizona's windy days and go fly a kite. If you don't already own one, you can purchase a kite at the Flagstaff Visitor Center on Kite Day and fly it in one of several designated city parks. ⊕ *www.flagstaffarizona.org.*

June

Grand Canyon Star Party. Lectures and nightly telescope sessions take place at both the South and North rims over the course of eight days. The event is free and open to the general public with park entrance fee. ⊕ *www.nps.gov/grca.*

Flagstaff Folk Festival. This weekend-long folk music festival features more than 70 acts on three stages, musical workshops, and informal jamming sessions. Admission is $10 per person or $15 per family. ⊕ *flagfolkfest.org.*

Williams Historic Route 66 Car Show. Every June, classic cars rumble into Williams. Tour the displayed cars, watch a parade of classic cars, and listen to live music.

July

4th of July, Flagstaff. Flagstaff goes all out, honoring our nation's founding with a parade, juried arts and craft show, free pops concert, and a patriotic laser light show. ⊕ www.flagstaffarizona.org.

4th of July, Williams. Williams celebrates the Fourth with a parade, ice cream social, and fire-safe firework display, conditions permitting.

August

Hopi Arts & Cultural Festival. This weekend-long all-Hopi art festival showcases traditional and contemporary artwork, baskets, pottery, and other fine arts as dancers perform tribal dances throughout the day. ⊕ hopifestival.com.

September

Coconino County Fair. One of northern Arizona's largest events, the Coconino County Fair features live music, livestock shows, arts and crafts, cultural performances, carnival rides, and of course, carnival food favorites. ⊕ www.coconinocountyfair.com.

Grand Canyon Music Festival. Held at the Shrine of Ages amphitheater, it stages nearly a dozen concerts on three consecutive weekends. ⊕ grandcanyonmusicfest.org.

Pickin' in the Pines Bluegrass & Acoustic Music Festival. Attendees come from all over the Southwest and beyond to hear bluegrass, old-time music, Celtic, gypsy jazz, and other forms of acoustic music. ⊕ pickininthepines.org.

October

Flagstaff Oktoberfest. Enjoy beer, bratwurst, pretzels, and polka in Wheeler Park the first weekend in October. ⊕ flagstaffoktoberfest.com.

December

The Great Pinecone Drop. Flagstaff kicks off the New Year with the traditional lowering of a giant pinecone from the top of the Weatherford Hotel, followed by fireworks. ⊕ pineconedrop.com.

Polar Express. The Grand Canyon Railway brings the children's classic *The Polar Express* by Chris Van Allsburg to life. Kids sip hot chocolate and munch on cookies as they head to the North Pole, where Santa and his reindeer await. ⊕ www.thetrain.com/events/polar-express.

Contacts

Air

Flagstaff Pulliam Airport (FLG). ✉ *6200 S. Pulliam Dr., Flagstaff* ☎ *928/213–2930* ⊕ *flyflagstaffaz.com.* **Grand Canyon National Park (GCN).** ✉ *1542 Liberator Dr., Grand Canyon, Grand Canyon Village* ☎ *928/638–2446* ⊕ *www.azdot.gov/about/grand-canyon-airport.* **Grand Canyon West Airport (GCW).** ✉ *5001 Diamond Bar Rd., Peach Springs* ☎ *928/769–2419* ⊕ *grandcanyonwest.com.* **Harry Reid International Airport (LAS).** ✉ *5757 Wayne Newton Blvd., Las Vegas* ☎ *702/261–5211* ⊕ *www.harryreidairport. com.* **Page Municipal Airport (PGA).** ✉ *238 10th Ave., Page* ☎ *928/645–4240* ⊕ *cityofpage. org/departments/airport.* **Phoenix Sky Harbor International Airport (PHX).** ✉ *3400 E. Sky Harbor Blvd., Phoenix* ☎ *602/273–3300* ⊕ *www.skyharbor.com.* **St. George Regional Airport (SGU).** ✉ *4550 S. Airport Pkwy., St. George* ☎ *435/627–4080* ⊕ *www.flysgu.com.*

Lodging

CAMPING PERMITS
Coconino National Forest. ☎ *877/444–6777* ⊕ *www. recreation.gov.* **Grand Canyon National Park Back Country Information Center.** ✉ *1824 S. Thompson St., Suite 201, Flagstaff* ☎ *928/638–7875* ⊕ *www.nps.gov/grca/planyourvisit/backcountry-permit.htm.* **Havasupai Tourism Enterprise.** ⊕ *www.havasupaireservations. com.* **Kaibab National Forest.** ☎ *(877) 444–6777* ⊕ *www. recreation.gov.* **Xanterra Parks and Resorts.** ☎ *(888) 297–2757* ⊕ *www.grandcanyonlodges. com.*

⚠ Emergencies

Grand Canyon National Park Emergency Services. ☎ *928/638–7688* ⊕ *www.nps.gov/grca/emergency.htm.*

Car

RV RENTALS Cruise America.
☎ 800/671–8042 ⊕ www.
cruiseamerica.com.

Bus

**SHUTTLE BUS Groome Transpor-
tation.** ✉ 2646 E. Huntington
Dr., Flagstaff ☎ 928/350–8466
⊕ groometransportation.
com. **Xanterra Transportation.**
☎ 888/297–2757 ⊕ www.
grandcanyonlodges.com.

Taxi

Williams Taxi and Shuttle.
✉ Williams ☎ 928/635–1111
⊕ www.williamstaxi.com.
Xanterra Taxi Service. ✉ Grand
Canyon ☎ 928/638–2631
⊕ www.grandcanyonlodges.
com.

Train

Amtrak. ☎ 800/872–7245
⊕ www.amtrak.com. **Grand
Canyon Railway.** ✉ 233 N.
Grand Canyon Blvd., Williams
☎ 928/635–4010, 800/843–
8724 ⊕ www.thetrain.com.

Visitor Information

Flagstaff Visitor Center.
✉ One E. Rte. 66, Flagstaff
☎ 928/213–2951, 800/379–
0065 ⊕ www.flagstaffarizona.
org. **Grand Canyon National Park.**
☎ 928/638–7888 ⊕ www.nps.
gov/grca. **Grand Canyon West.**
⊕ grandcanyonwest.com.
Havasupai Tourism Enterprise.
⊕ www.havasupaireservations.
com. **Hualapai Tribe.** ⊕ hualap-
ai-nsn.gov.

Chapter 3

THE SOUTH RIM

Updated by
Teresa Bitler

⛰ Camping   🛏 Hotels   🎿 Activities   👁 Scenery   👥 Crowds

★★★☆☆   ★★★☆☆   ★★★★★   ★★★★★   ★★★★★

WELCOME TO THE SOUTH RIM

TOP REASONS TO GO

★ **Iconic views:** Mather, Hopi, Yavapai, and Yaki Points—where photographers take some of the most common images of the Grand Canyon—are all on the South Rim.

★ **Mule rides:** A bucket list–worthy adventure, mule rides to the bottom of the canyon are available only from the South Rim. Visitors short on time can take a two-hour ride along the rim instead.

★ **Tours:** In addition to mule rides, the South Rim offers air, 4x4, bus, and guided bicycle tours as well as guided hikes. Rafting trips often end at Phantom Ranch, and rafters hike out of the canyon to the South Rim.

★ **Continuing education:** Adults and kids can have fun learning, thanks to free park-sponsored hikes and interpretive programs. The Grand Canyon Conservancy offers more in-depth programs for a fee.

★ **Architecture:** Hopi House, Hermits Rest, Lookout Studio, and Desert View Watchtower bear witness to the architectural genius of Mary Jane Colter.

Roughly 90 percent of the six million people who visit Grand Canyon National Park annually do so at its South Rim. It can get crowded, especially during the summer, but it also has more tours, programs, hotels, and restaurants than the North Rim or Grand Canyon West.

1 Hermits Rest. The western-most viewpoint on the South Rim is also the shuttle's last stop and where you'll pick up the

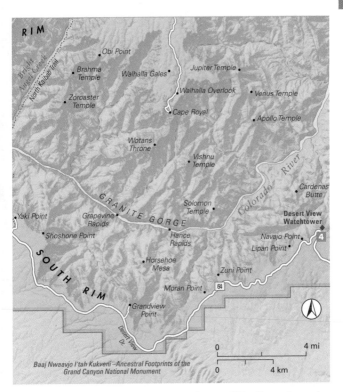

Baaj Nwaavjo I'tah Kukveni –Ancestral Footprints of the Grand Canyon National Monument

Hermit Trailhead. You can buy souvenirs and snacks in the Mary Jane Colter–designed stone building here.

2 Grand Canyon Village. The epicenter of the South Rim, this is where you'll find the park's lodging, restaurants, stores, and plenty of trailheads. The train depot is here, too, and Yaki Barn, where the mule rides originate.

3 Mather Point. For most visitors, Mather Point is their first look at the canyon. It's also where you'll be directed to park and take the shuttle throughout the park. A visitor center and gift shop are located off the parking lot.

4 Desert View Watchtower. This watchtower overlooks the Colorado River, painted canyon walls, and distant Navajo lands. It was designed by Mary Jane Colter to look like ancient Puebloan towers found throughout the Southwest.

When Lt. Joseph Ives visited the South Rim of the Grand Canyon on an exploratory U.S. War Department expedition in 1857, he declared it to be "altogether valueless."

"Ours has been the first and will doubtless be the last party of whites to visit this profitless locality," Ives remarked. "It seems intended by nature that the Colorado River, along the greater portion of its lonely and majestic way, shall be forever unvisited and undisturbed." He was wrong. Of the six million people who visit the Grand Canyon each year, approximately 90% throng the South Rim's lodges, restaurants, and breathtaking viewpoints. Visiting during peak summer weekends and holidays requires patience and a tolerance for crowds. Even while jostling for a spot at the most popular viewpoints, most visitors are enthralled by the sheer scope of the deepest, most stunning canyon on the planet. Visiting in the off-season—including winter, when the snow mantles the landscape and contrasts with the vibrant colors of the canyon—offers a more intimate experience.

Most people don't give the canyon enough time, flitting quickly from viewpoint to viewpoint near the main lodge. Many drive to the main visitor center then take the 25-mile Desert View Drive, which follows the rim and offers frequent viewpoints. But even during the peak times you can find some solitude from the pressing crowds. A bus shuttles passengers to the less visited and less crowded viewpoints to the west of the main lodge. You can also walk down several different trails, although the steep climb and high elevation can pose problems for people who aren't in shape or have heart or respiratory problems.

Another option is to start from the main lodge and stroll along the mostly paved Rim Trail. Crowds drop off sharply as soon as you start walking, even during the busy seasons. Try to arrange your schedule to take in at least one sunrise or sunset. The light of midday flattens even the Grand Canyon, but early and late light make the sandstone cliffs glow and fill the canyon's depths with shadow. The drama of the canyon is enhanced with a glimpse of one of the endangered California condors, which were reintroduced to their historical canyon habitat in 1996. The condors often visit the South Rim, although watchful biologists try to shoo them away to prevent them from getting used to human beings.

Planning

When to Go

There's no bad time to visit the canyon, though some of the busiest times of the year are summer and spring break. Visiting during those peak seasons, as well as holidays, requires patience and a tolerance for crowds. You'll also want to start planning your vacation at those times more than a year before, as lodging and activities book up well in advance. In contrast, the winter months at the South Rim are quieter, but some restaurants, services, and outfitters either close or curtail their services. If weather is a concern, take note that the South Rim averages 58 inches of snow annually, with temperatures dipping below freezing at night November through April. Spring and early summer are generally the driest time of the year, but by late summer, monsoon season is in full force with clouds building from midmorning until they unleash powerful thunderstorms in the late afternoon.

Getting Here and Around

AIR

Scenic Airlines (☎ 702/638–3300 ⊕ www.scenic.com) flies regularly from Harry Reid International Airport in Las Vegas to the **Grand Canyon National Park Airport** in Tusayan (☎ 928/638–2446). **Maverick Airlines** (☎ 702/728–4241) offers charter flights.

CAR

You can enter the park at the South Rim through its south or east entrance. Either way, your route begins in Flagstaff. To use the south entrance (the most common one), take U.S. 180 northwest out of Flagstaff to Highway 64, which will take you directly into the park, and turn left. You can also access the south entrance by exiting Interstate 40 where it meets Highway 64 and heading north on Highway 64 into the park. To enter from the east, take Highway 89 northeast out of Flagstaff and continue to Cameron, then turn left at Highway 64.

IN-PARK SHUTTLES

The South Rim is open to car traffic year-round, though access to Hermits Rest is limited to shuttle buses part of the year. There are four free shuttle routes. The Hermits Rest Route operates March through November between Grand Canyon Village and Hermits Rest. The Village Route operates year-round in the village area, stopping at lodgings, the general store, and the Grand Canyon

Visitor Center. The Kaibab Rim Route goes from the visitor center to five viewpoints, including the Yavapai Geology Museum and Yaki Point (where cars are not permitted). The Tusayan Route runs Memorial Day to Labor Day, bringing visitors staying in Tusayan to the Grand Canyon Visitor Center. The Hiker's Express shuttles hikers from the village to the South Kaibab Trailhead three times each morning (twice during December through February).

■TIP→ **In summer, South Rim roads are congested, and it's easier and sometimes required to park your car and take the free shuttle.**

Running from one hour before sunrise until one hour after sunset, shuttles in the park arrive every 15 to 30 minutes at 30 clearly marked stops. The shuttle between Tusayan and the park runs from 8 am to 9:30 pm, arriving every 20 minutes.

TAXI AND SHUTTLE

Although there's no public transportation into the Grand Canyon, you can hire a taxi through Grand Canyon National Park Lodges (☎ *928/638–2822* ⊕ *www.grandcanyonlodges.com*) to take you to or from the Grand Canyon Airport. There is currently no taxi service from Flagstaff to the South Rim. However, shuttle service is available from Flagstaff through Groome Transportation (☎ *928/350–8466* ⊕ *groometransportation.com/arizona*) and from the South Rim to the North Rim through the Trans Canyon Shuttle (☎ *928/638–2820* ⊕ *www.trans-canyonshuttle.com*).

TRAIN

Grand Canyon Railway. There's no need to deal with all of the other drivers racing to the South Rim. Sit back and relax in the comfy train cars of the Grand Canyon Railway. Live music and storytelling enliven the trip as you journey through prairie, ranch, and national park to the log-cabin train station in Grand Canyon Village. You won't see the Grand Canyon from the train, but you can walk (¼ mile) to the rim or catch a shuttle to take it in at the park's scenic overlooks. The vintage train departs from the Williams Depot every morning and makes the 65-mile journey in 2¼ hours. You can do the round trip in a single day; however, it's a more relaxing and enjoyable strategy to stay for a night or two at the South Rim before returning to Williams. Fares run from $67 to $226 round-trip, not including park entry fee or tax. Add-ons, like snacks, may increase your fare, too, depending on the package booked. ☎ *800/843–8724, 928/635–4010* ⊕ *www.thetrain.com*.

Hotels

Accommodations at the South Rim include two "historic-rustic" facilities: El Tovar and Bright Angel Lodge & Cabins. The South Rim's architectural highlight, El Tovar has hosted dignitaries, including Theodore Roosevelt, Albert Einstein, and Oprah Winfrey, while Bright Angel Lodge is a registered National Historic Landmark. The other accommodations are motel-style lodges, and although they are relatively basic, they're comfortable. Of course, the most sought-after rooms have canyon views, and reservations are a must, especially during the busy summer season.

■ TIP→ **If you want to get your first choice (especially Bright Angel Lodge or El Tovar), make reservations as far in advance as possible; they're taken up to 13 months ahead. You might find a last-minute cancellation, but you shouldn't count on it.**

Although lodging at the South Rim will keep you close to the action, the frenetic activity and crowded facilities are off-putting to some. With short notice, the best time to find a room at the South Rim is in the winter. Or you can try your luck at Tusayan. Just outside the park's south entrance, the community has a number of large chain hotels.

Restaurants

At the South Rim, you can find everything from cafeteria food to creatively prepared Southwestern cuisine. There's even a coffeehouse with organic joe. The dress code is casual across the board, but El Tovar is your best option if you're looking to dress up a bit and thumb through an extensive wine list. For a more casual experience, the park has several picnic areas, but drinking water and restrooms aren't available at most of these spots.

During the summer, the restaurants on the South Rim can have long lines or long waits for a table. Another option is to leave the park and eat at one of the restaurants in Tusayan, minutes from the park's entrance. You can take a break, have a meal, and reenter the park.

⇨ *Hotel prices in the reviews are the lowest cost of a standard double room in high season. Restaurant prices in the reviews are the average cost of a main course at dinner, or if dinner is not served, at lunch.*

What It Costs in U.S. Dollars			
$	$$	$$$	$$$$
HOTELS			
under $120	$120–$175	$176–$250	over $250
RESTAURANTS			
under $12	$12–$20	$21–$30	over $30

Tours

Grand Canyon Conservancy Field Institute
GUIDED TOURS | Instructors lead guided educational tours, hikes around the canyon, and weekend programs at the South Rim. With more than 200 classes a year, tour topics include everything from archaeology and backcountry medicine to photography and natural history. Check online for a schedule and program prices. Private hikes can be arranged. Discounted classes are available for members; annual dues are $35. ⊠ *GCA Warehouse, 2–B Albright Ave., Grand Canyon Village* ☎ *928/638–2481, 800/858–2808* ⊕ *www.grandcanyon.org/fieldinstitute* 🎫 *From $235.*

Xanterra Motorcoach Tours
GUIDED TOURS | Narrated by knowledgeable guides, tours include the Hermits Rest Tour, which travels along the old wagon road built by the Santa Fe Railway; the Desert View Tour, which glimpses the Colorado River's rapids and stops at Lipan Point; Sunrise and Sunset tours; and combination tours. Children two and younger are free when accompanied by a paying adult. ☎ *303/297–2757, 888/297–2757* ⊕ *www.grandcanyonlodges.com* 🎫 *From $40.*

The South Rim

Sights

HISTORIC SIGHTS
Tusayan Ruin and Museum
INDIGENOUS SIGHT | This museum offers a quick orientation to the prehistoric and modern indigenous populations of the Grand Canyon and the Colorado Plateau, including an excavation of an 800-year-old Pueblo site. Of special interest are split-twig figurines dating back 2,000 to 4,000 years and other artifacts left behind by ancient cultures. A ranger leads daily interpretive tours of the

While the Grand Canyon is famous for its scenic hikes, the Tusayan museum is well worth a visit to check out its prehistoric artifacts.

Ancestral Pueblo village. ⊠ *Grand Canyon National Park* ⊕ *About 20 miles east of Grand Canyon Village on E. Rim Dr.* ☎ *928/638–7888* 🖾 *Free.*

PICNIC AREAS

Bring your picnic basket and enjoy dining alfresco surrounded by some of the most beautiful backdrops in the country. Note that some of these spots do not have restrooms or water available.

Buggeln, 15 miles east of Grand Canyon Village on Desert View Drive, has some secluded, shady spots.

Grandview Point has, as the name implies, grand vistas; it's 12 miles east of the village on Desert View Drive.

SCENIC DRIVES
Desert View Drive

SCENIC DRIVE | This heavily traveled 25-mile stretch of road follows the rim from the east entrance to Grand Canyon Village. Starting from the less congested entry near Desert View, road warriors can get their first glimpse of the canyon from the 70-foot-tall watchtower, the top of which provides the highest viewpoint on the South Rim. Six developed canyon viewpoints in addition to unmarked pullouts, the remains of an Ancestral Puebloan dwelling at the Tusayan Ruin and Museum, and the secluded and lovely Buggeln picnic area make for great stops along the South Rim. The Kaibab Rim Route shuttle bus travels a short section of Desert View Drive and takes 50 minutes to ride round-trip without

Grand Canyon South Rim

PALISADES OF THE DESERT

NORTH RIM

WALHALLA PLATEAU

Cape Royal Road

SOUTH RIM

GRANITE GORGE

UPPER GRANITE GORGE

Colorado River

Chuar Butte
Siegfried Pyre
Venus Temple
Apollo Temple
Cardenas Butte
Jupiter Temple
Walhalla Overlook
Cape Royal
Obi Point
Walhalla Glades
Wotans Throne
Vishnu Temple
Solomon Temple
Brahma Temple
Zoroaster Temple
Clear Creek Trail
North Kaibab Trail
Bright Angel Trail
Wildross Trail
Isis Temple
Shiva Temple
Osiris Temple
Tower of Ra
Point Sublime
Diana Temple
Boucher Rapids
Dripping Springs
Hermits Rest
Pima Point
Hermit Trail
Hermit Road
The Abyss
Mohave Point
Hopi Point
Granite Rapids
Horn Creek Rapids
Powell Point and Memorial
Maricopa Point
Yavapai Point
Trailview Overlook
Bright Angel Trailhead
Phantom Ranch
South Kaibab Trail
Yaki Point
Shoshone Point
Grapevine Rapids
Grandview Trail
Horseshoe Mesa
Hance Rapids
Solomon Temple
Moran Point
Grandview Point
Desert View Drive
Zuni Point
Lipan Point
Navajo Point
Tusayan Ruin and Museum
Desert View and Watchtower
East Entrance
Cardenas Butte

North Rim Visitor Center

Grand Canyon Village

See Grand Canyon Village map

Mather Point

Lookout Studio

South Entrance

Tusayan

Grand Canyon Airport

TO FLAGSTAFF, WILLIAMS

TO CAMERON AND NORTH RIM

Colorado River

64
180
64

4 mi
4 km
0

Baaj Nwaavjo I'tah Kukveni—Ancestral Footprints of the

KEY

🏠 Ranger Station
⛺ Campground
🍴 Picnic Area
🍽 Restaurant
🏨 Lodge
······· Trails
= = = Dirt Roads

Best Grand Canyon Views

The best times of day to see the canyon are before 10 am or after 4 pm, when the angle of the sun brings out the colors of the rock, and clouds and shadows add dimension. Colors deepen dramatically among the contrasting layers of the canyon walls just before and during sunrise and sunset.

Hopi Point is the top spot on the South Rim to watch the sunset; **Yaki** and **Pima** Points also offer vivid views. For a grand sunrise, try **Mather** or **Yaki Point.**

■TIP→ Arrive at least 30 minutes early for sunrise views and as much as 90 minutes for sunset views at these points.

For another point of view, take a leisurely stroll along the Rim Trail and watch the color change along with the views. Timetables are posted at park visitor centers.

getting off at any of the stops: Grand Canyon Visitor Center, South Kaibab Trailhead, Yaki Point, Pipe Creek Vista, Mather Point, and Yavapai Geology Museum. ⊠ *Grand Canyon National Park.*

Hermit Road
SCENIC DRIVE | The Santa Fe Company built Hermit Road, formerly known as West Rim Drive, in 1912 as a scenic tour route. Nine overlooks dot this 7-mile stretch, each worth a visit. The road is filled with hairpin turns, so make sure you adhere to posted speed limits. A 1½-mile Greenway trail offers easy access to cyclists looking to enjoy the original 1912 Hermit Rim Road. From March through November, Hermit Road is closed to private auto traffic because of congestion; during this period, a free shuttle bus carries visitors to all the overlooks. Riding the bus round-trip without getting off at any of the viewpoints takes 80 minutes; the return trip stops only at Hermits Rest, Pima, Mohave, and Powell Points. ⊠ *Grand Canyon National Park.*

SCENIC STOPS
The Abyss
VIEWPOINT | At an elevation of 6,720 feet, the Abyss is one of the most awesome stops on Hermit Road, revealing a sheer drop of 3,000 feet to the Tonto Platform, a wide terrace of Tapeats sandstone about two-thirds of the way down the canyon. From the Abyss you'll also see several isolated sandstone columns, the largest of which is called The Monument. ⊠ *Grand Canyon National Park* ✛ *About 5 miles west of Hermit Rd. Junction on Hermit Rd.*

Climb the 85 steps of the circular stone Watchtower to take in 360-degree views of the national park.

Desert View Watchtower

VIEWPOINT | From the top of the 70-foot stone-and-mortar watchtower with its 360-degree views, even the muted hues of the distant Painted Desert to the east and the Vermilion Cliffs rising from a high plateau near the Utah border are visible. In the chasm below, angling to the north toward Marble Canyon, an imposing stretch of the Colorado River reveals itself. Up several flights of stairs, the watchtower houses a glass-enclosed observatory with telescopes. ⊠ *Grand Canyon National Park* ✛ *Just north of East Entrance Station on Desert View Dr.* ☎ *928/638–7888* ⊕ *www. nps.gov/grca* ☒ *Free.*

Grandview Point

VIEWPOINT | At an elevation of 7,399 feet, the view from here is one of the finest in the canyon. To the northeast is a group of dominant buttes, including Krishna Shrine, Vishnu Temple, Rama Shrine, and Sheba Temple. A short stretch of the Colorado River is also visible. Directly below the point, and accessible by the steep and rugged Grandview Trail, is Horseshoe Mesa, where you can see remnants of Last Chance Copper Mine. ⊠ *Grand Canyon National Park* ✛ *About 12 miles east of Grand Canyon Village on Desert View Dr.*

Hermits Rest

VIEWPOINT | This westernmost viewpoint and Hermit Trail, which descends from it, were named for "hermit" Louis Boucher, a 19th-century French-Canadian prospector who had a number of mining claims and a roughly built home down in the canyon. The trail served as the original mule ride down to Hermit Camp beginning in 1914. Views from here include Hermit Rapids and the towering cliffs of the Supai and Redwall formations. You can buy curios and snacks in the stone building at Hermits Rest. ⊠ *Grand Canyon National Park* ✥ *About 8 miles west of Hermit Rd. Junction on Hermit Rd.*

★ Hopi Point

VIEWPOINT | From this elevation of 7,071 feet, you can see a large section of the Colorado River; although it appears as a thin line, the river is nearly 350 feet wide. The overlook extends farther into the canyon than any other point on Hermit Road. The incredible unobstructed views make this a popular place to watch the sunset.

Across the canyon to the north is Shiva Temple. In 1937 Harold Anthony of the American Museum of Natural History led an expedition to the rock formation in the belief that it supported life that had been cut off from the rest of the canyon. Imagine the expedition members' surprise when they found an empty Kodak film box on top of the temple—it had been left behind by Emery Kolb, who felt slighted for not having been invited to join Anthony's tour.

Directly below Hopi Point lies Dana Butte, named for a prominent 19th-century geologist. In 1919 an entrepreneur proposed connecting Hopi Point, Dana Butte, and the Tower of Set across the river with an aerial tramway, a technically feasible plan that fortunately has not been realized. ⊠ *Grand Canyon National Park* ✥ *About 4 miles west of Hermit Rd. Junction on Hermit Rd.*

Lipan Point

VIEWPOINT | Here, at the canyon's widest point, you can get an astonishing visual profile of the gorge's geologic history, with a view of every eroded layer of the canyon and one of the longest visible stretches of Colorado River. The spacious panorama stretches to the Vermilion Cliffs on the northeastern horizon and features a multitude of imaginatively named spires, buttes, and temples—intriguing rock formations named after their resemblance to ancient pyramids. You can also see Unkar Delta, where a creek joins the Colorado to form powerful rapids and a broad beach. Ancestral Pueblo farmers worked the Unkar Delta for hundreds of years, growing corn, beans, and melons. ⊠ *Grand Canyon National Park* ✥ *About 25 miles east of Grand Canyon Village on Desert View Dr.*

Did You Know?

Hopi Point was originally named Rowes Point after businessman Sanford Rowe, who was the first person to offer guided trips into the area. It was later renamed Hopi Point to honor the Hopi tribe. The unobstructed views it offers makes it a popular sunset-viewing spot.

Mather Point is one of the most popular lookout points on the Grand Canyon's South Rim.

★ Mather Point

VIEWPOINT | You'll likely get your first glimpse of the canyon from this viewpoint, one of the most impressive and accessible (next to the main visitor center plaza) on the South Rim. Named for the National Park Service's first director, Stephen Mather, this spot yields extraordinary views of the Grand Canyon, including deep into the inner gorge and numerous buttes: Wotans Throne, Brahma Temple, and Zoroaster Temple, among others. ⊠ *Near Grand Canyon Visitor Center, Grand Canyon National Park* ☎ *928/638–7888* ⊕ *www.nps.gov/grca.*

Moran Point

VIEWPOINT | This point was named for American landscape artist Thomas Moran, who was especially fond of the play of light and shadows from this location. He first visited the canyon with John Wesley Powell in 1873. "Thomas Moran's name, more than any other, with the possible exception of Major Powell's, is to be associated with the Grand Canyon," wrote noted canyon photographer Ellsworth Kolb. It's fitting that Moran Point is a favorite spot of photographers and painters. ⊠ *Grand Canyon National Park* ⊹ *About 17 miles east of Grand Canyon Village on Desert View Dr.*

Trailview Overlook

VIEWPOINT | Look down on a dramatic view of the Bright Angel and Plateau Point trails as they zigzag down the canyon. In the deep gorge to the north flows Bright Angel Creek, one of the region's few permanent tributary streams of the Colorado River. Toward the south is an unobstructed view of the distant San Francisco Peaks, as well as Bill Williams Mountain and Red Butte. ⊠ *Grand Canyon National Park* ⊹ *About 2 miles west of Hermit Rd. Junction on Hermit Rd.*

Yaki Point

VIEWPOINT | Take the Kaibab Rim shuttle here (no private vehicles are allowed) for an exceptional view of Wotans Throne, a flat-top butte named by François Matthes, a U.S. Geological Survey scientist who developed the first topographical map of the Grand Canyon. The overlook juts out over the canyon, providing unobstructed views of inner-canyon rock formations, South Rim cliffs, and Clear Creek Canyon. It's one of the best places on the South Rim to watch the sunrise or sunset. About a mile south is the trailhead for the South Kaibab Trail. ⊠ *Grand Canyon National Park* ⊹ *4 miles east of Grand Canyon Village on Desert View Dr.*

★ Yavapai Point

VIEWPOINT | Dominated by the Yavapai Geology Museum and Observation Station, this point displays panoramic views of the mighty gorge through a wall of windows. Exhibits at the museum include videos of the canyon floor and the Colorado River, a scaled diorama of the canyon with national park boundaries, fossils, and rock fragments used to re-create the complex layers of the canyon walls, and a display on the natural forces used to carve the chasm. Dig even deeper into Grand Canyon geology with free daily ranger programs. This point is also a good location to watch the sunset. ⊠ *Grand Canyon Village* ⊹ *1 mile east of Market Plaza.*

TRAILS

★ Bright Angel Trail

TRAIL | This well-maintained trail is one of the most scenic (and busiest) hiking paths from the South Rim to the bottom of the canyon (9.6 miles each way). Rest houses are equipped with water at the 1½- and 3-mile points from May through September and at Havasupai Gardens (4 miles) year-round. Water is also available at Bright Angel Campground, 9¼ miles below the trailhead. Plateau Point, on a spur trail about 1½ miles below Havasupai Gardens, is as far as you should attempt to go on a day hike; the round-trip will take six to nine hours.

Bright Angel Trail is the easiest of all the footpaths into the canyon, but because the climb out from the bottom is an ascent of 5,510 feet, the trip should be attempted only by those in good physical condition and should be avoided in midsummer due to extreme heat. The top of the trail can be icy in winter. Originally a bighorn sheep path and later used by the Havasupai, the trail was

Did You Know?

Originally a bighorn sheep path and later used by the Havasupai, Bright Angel Trail was widened late in the 19th century for prospectors and is now used for both mule and foot traffic. Note that mule trains have the right-of-way.

widened late in the 19th century for prospectors and is now used for both mule and foot traffic. Also note that mule trains have the right-of-way—and sometimes leave unpleasant surprises in your path. *Moderate.* ⊠ *Grand Canyon National Park* ✧ *Trailhead: Kolb Studio, Hermit Rd.*

Clear Creek Trail

HIKING & WALKING | This multiday, 9-mile hike (each way) departs from Phantom Ranch at the bottom of the canyon and crosses the Tonto Platform to Clear Creek, where drinking water is usually available but should be treated. You can continue an additional 6 miles to the Colorado River and, from that point, it's another 5 miles to Cheyava Falls, which flows in the spring after a winter of heavy snows. These last two legs extend the hike several days and require some scrambling and free climbing. Because the slope is south-facing and has no shade, this trail shouldn't be attempted in the summer. *Moderate.* ⊠ *Grand Canyon National Park* ✧ *Trailhead: Phantom Ranch.*

Grandview Trail

TRAIL | Accessible from the parking area at Grandview Point, the trailhead is at 7,400 feet. The path heads steeply down into the canyon for 3 miles to the junction and campsite at East Horseshoe Mesa Trail. Classified as a wilderness trail, the route is aggressive and not as heavily traveled as some of the more well-known trails, such as Bright Angel and Hermit. There is no water available along the trail, which follows a steep descent to 4,900 feet at Horseshoe Mesa, where Hopi Indians once collected mineral paints. Hike 0.7 mile farther to Page Spring, a reliable water source year-round. Parts of this trail are icy in winter, and traction crampons are mandatory. *Difficult.* ⊠ *Grand Canyon National Park* ✧ *Trailhead: Grandview Point, Desert View Dr.*

Hermit Trail

TRAIL | Beginning on the South Rim just west of Hermits Rest (and 7 miles west of Grand Canyon Village), this steep, unmaintained, 9.7-mile (one-way) trail drops more than 5,000 feet to Hermit Creek, which usually flows year-round. It's a strenuous hike back up and is recommended for experienced long-distance hikers only; plan for six to nine hours. There's an abundance of lush growth and wildlife, including desert bighorn sheep, along this trail. The trail descends from the trailhead at 6,640 feet to the Colorado River at 2,300 feet. Day hikers should not go past Santa Maria Spring at 5,000 feet (a 5-mile round-trip).

Tips for Avoiding the Crowds

It's hard to commune with nature while you're searching for a parking place, dodging video cameras, and stepping away from strollers. However, this scenario is likely only during the peak summer months. One option is to bypass the South Rim and head to the North Rim instead. Or avoid Grand Canyon National Park altogether in favor of the West Rim of the canyon or tribal lands of the Hualapai and Havasupai. If only the park itself will do, the following tips will help you to keep your distance and your cool.

Take Another Route

Avoid road rage by choosing a different route to the South Rim, forgoing traditional Highway 64 and U.S. 180 from Flagstaff. Take U.S. 89 north from Flagstaff instead, passing near Sunset Crater and Wupatki national monuments. When you reach the junction with Highway 64, take a break at Cameron Trading Post (1 mile north of the junction)—or stay overnight. This is a good place to shop for Native American artifacts, souvenirs, and the usual postcards, dream catchers, recordings, and T-shirts. There are also high-quality Navajo rugs, jewelry, and other authentic handicrafts, and you can sample Navajo tacos. U.S. 64 to the west takes you directly to the park's east entrance; the scenery along the Little Colorado River gorge en route is eye-popping. It's 55 miles from Cameron Trading Post to the main visitor center and Mather Point.

Explore the North Rim

Although the North Rim is just 10 miles across from the South Rim, the trip to get there by car is a five-hour drive of 215 miles. At first it might not sound like the trip would be worth it, but the payoff is huge. Along the way, you'll travel through some of the prettiest parts of the state and be granted even more stunning views than those on the more easily accessible South Rim. Those who make the North Rim trip often insist it has the canyon's most beautiful views and best hiking. To get to the North Rim from Flagstaff, take U.S. 89 north past Cameron, turning left onto U.S. 89A at Bitter Springs. En route you'll pass the area known as Vermilion Cliffs. At Jacob Lake, take Highway 67 directly to the Grand Canyon North Rim. North Rim services are closed from November through mid-May because of heavy snow, but in summer months and early fall, it's a wonderful way to beat the crowds at the South Rim.

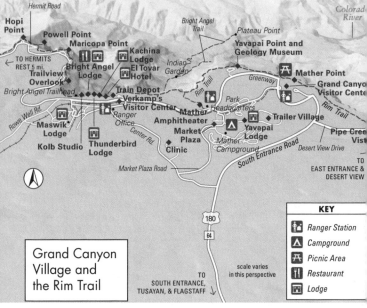

Grand Canyon
Village and
the Rim Trail

KEY

🏕	Ranger Station
⛺	Campground
🏕	Picnic Area
🍴	Restaurant
🏨	Lodge

scale varies
in this perspective

For much of the year, no water is available along the way; ask a
park ranger about the availability of water at Santa Maria Spring
and Hermit Creek before you set out. All water from these sourc-
es should be treated before drinking. The route leads down to the
Colorado River and has inspiring views of Hermit Gorge and the
Redwall and Supai formations. Six miles from the trailhead are the
ruins of Hermit Camp, which the Santa Fe Railroad ran as a tourist
camp from 1911 until 1930. *Difficult.* ✉ *Grand Canyon National
Park* ⚓ *Trailhead: Hermits Rest, Hermits Rd.*

★ Rim Trail

TRAIL | The South Rim's most popular walking path is the 12.8-
mile (one-way) Rim Trail, which runs along the edge of the canyon
from Pipe Creek Vista (the first overlook on Desert View Drive) to
Hermits Rest. This walk, which is paved to Maricopa Point and
for the last 1½ miles to Hermits Rest, visits several of the South
Rim's historic landmarks. Allow anywhere from 15 minutes to a
full day, depending on how much of the trail you want to cover;
the Rim Trail is an ideal day hike, as it varies only a few hundred
feet in elevation from Mather Point (7,120 feet) to the trailhead at
Hermits Rest (6,650 feet). The trail can also be accessed from several spots in Grand Canyon Village and from the major viewpoints

Grand Canyon History

The Grand Canyon's oldest layers date back to 1.8 billion years ago. The geological wonder is a prime example of arid-land erosion.

Indigenous groups inhabited the land much earlier than the first European explorers to "find" it in 1540. In fact, there's evidence of humans from 12,000 years ago. Hualapai and Havasupai are among the tribes that still live in the area.

An explorer of the American West, John Wesley Powell, bestowed the name "Grand" to the canyon as he led his expedition down the Colorado River in 1869.

In 1901, train tracks were completed to Grand Canyon Village, enabling more visitors to see the Grand Canyon.

Teddy Roosevelt, a champion for protecting land with government funding, gave the Grand Canyon National Monument status in 1908.

The Grand Canyon became America's 17th National Park in 1919 under President Woodrow Wilson.

along Hermit Road, which are serviced by shuttle buses during the busy summer months. On the Rim Trail, water is available only in the Grand Canyon Village area and at Hermits Rest. *Easy.* ⊠ *Grand Canyon National Park.*

South Kaibab Trail

TRAIL | This trail starts near Yaki Point, 4 miles east of Grand Canyon Village, and is accessible via the free shuttle bus.

Because the route is so steep (and sometimes icy in winter)—descending from the trailhead at 7,260 feet down to 2,480 feet at the Colorado River—many hikers take this trail down, then ascend via the less demanding Bright Angel Trail. Allow four to six hours to reach the Colorado River on this 6.4-mile trek. At the river, the trail crosses a suspension bridge and runs on to Phantom Ranch. Along the trail there is no water and little shade. There are no campgrounds, though there are portable toilets at Cedar Ridge (6,320 feet), 1½ miles from the trailhead. An emergency phone is available at the Tipoff, 4.6 miles down the trail (3 miles past Cedar Ridge). The trail corkscrews down through some spectacular geology. Look for (but don't remove) fossils in the limestone when taking water breaks. *Difficult.* ⊠ *Grand Canyon National Park* ✛ *Trailhead: Yaki Point Rd., off Desert View Dr.*

VISITOR CENTERS

Desert View Information Center

VISITOR CENTER | Near the Desert View Watchtower, this nonprofit Grand Canyon Association store and information center has a nice selection of books, park pamphlets, gifts, and educational materials. It's also a handy place to pick up maps and info if you enter the park at the eastern entrance. All sales from the Association stores go to support park programs. ⊠ *Eastern entrance, Grand Canyon National Park* ☎ *800/858–2808, 928/638–7888.*

Grand Canyon Verkamp's Visitor Center

VISITOR CENTER | This small visitor center is named for the Verkamp family, who operated a curios shop on the South Rim for more than a hundred years. The building serves as an official visitor center, ranger station (get your Junior Ranger badges here), bookstore, and museum, with compelling exhibits on the Verkamps and other pioneers in this region. ⊠ *Desert View Dr., Grand Canyon Village* ✛ *Across from El Tovar Hotel* ☎ *928/638–7146.*

Grand Canyon Visitor Center

VISITOR CENTER | The park's main orientation center provides pamphlets and resources to help plan your visit. It also holds engaging interpretive exhibits on the park. Rangers are on hand to answer questions and aid in planning canyon excursions. A daily schedule of ranger-led hikes and evening lectures is available, and a 20-minute film about the history, geology, and wildlife of the canyon plays every 30 minutes in the theater. The bicycle rental office, a small café, and a huge gift store are also in this complex. It's a five-minute walk from here to Mather Point, or a short ride on the shuttle bus, which can take you into Grand Canyon Village. The visitor center is also accessible from the village via a leisurely 2-mile walk on the Greenway Trail, a paved pathway that meanders through the forest. ⊠ *East side of Grand Canyon Village, 450 Hwy. 64, Grand Canyon* ☎ *928/638–7888.*

Yavapai Geology Museum

VISITOR CENTER | Learn about the geology of the canyon at this museum and bookstore that doubles as a visitor center. You can also catch the park shuttle bus or pick up information for the Rim Trail here. The views of the canyon and Phantom Ranch from inside this historic building are stupendous. ⊠ *1 mile east of Market Plaza, Grand Canyon Village* ☎ *928/638–7890.*

🍴 Restaurants

Arizona Steakhouse

$$$$ | **STEAKHOUSE** | The canyon views from this casual Southwestern-style steak house are the best of any restaurant at the South Rim. The dinner menu leans toward steak-house dishes, while lunch is primarily salads and sandwiches with a Southwestern twist. **Known for:** views of the Grand Canyon; Southwestern fare; local craft beers and wines. $ *Average main: $35* ✉ *Bright Angel Lodge, 9 N. Village Loop Dr., Grand Canyon Village* ☎ *928/638–2631* ⊕ *www.grandcanyonlodges.com.*

★ El Tovar Dining Room

$$$$ | **SOUTHWESTERN** | This cozy room of dark wood beams and stone, nestled in the historic El Tovar Lodge, dates to 1905. Gourmet classics such as duck, lamb, and salmon are on the menu, which focuses on locally sourced and organic ingredients. **Known for:** historic setting with canyon views; local and organic ingredients; fine dining that's worth the splurge. $ *Average main: $37* ✉ *El Tovar Hotel, 1 El Tovar Rd., Grand Canyon Village* ☎ *928/638–2631* ⊕ *www.grandcanyonlodges.com.*

Fred Harvey Burger

$$$ | **SOUTHWESTERN** | **FAMILY** | Open for lunch and dinner, this casual café at Bright Angel Lodge serves basics like salads, sandwiches, and burgers. Harvey House favorites like strip steak and spaghetti round out the menu. **Known for:** reasonably priced American fare for a national park; family-friendly menu and setting; some limited vegetarian and gluten-free options. $ *Average main: $26* ✉ *Bright Angel Lodge, Desert View Dr., Grand Canyon Village* ☎ *928/638–2631* ⊕ *www.grandcanyonlodges.com.*

Maswik Food Court

$$ | **AMERICAN** | **FAMILY** | You can get BBQ, hot sandwiches, hot dogs, or Mexican fare at this food court. The adjacent Maswik Pizza Pub serves pizza by the slice and wine and beer. **Known for:** something for everyone; cafeteria-style dining; pizza to go. $ *Average main: $15* ✉ *Maswik Lodge, South Village Loop Dr., Grand Canyon Village* ⊕ *www.grandcanyonlodges.com.*

Yavapai Dining Hall

$$$ | **AMERICAN** | **FAMILY** | If you don't have time for full-service, the restaurant in Yavapai Lodge offers cafeteria-style dining for breakfast and dinner, including beef brisket, pizza, baked chicken, and salmon. Wine and beer, including craft brews from nearby Flagstaff, are also on the menu; or enjoy drinks on the patio at the

The El Tovar Hotel's hunting-lodge atmosphere, convenient location, and elevated local cuisine make it one of the Park's best accomodations.

adjacent Yavapai Tavern, which serves lunch and dinner. **Known for:** quick bites or hearty meals; convenient dining in Market Plaza; patio with firepit at Yavapai Tavern. $ *Average main: $22* ⊠ *Yavapai Lodge, Yavapai Lodge Rd., Grand Canyon Village* ☎ *928/638–4001* ⊕ *www.visitgrandcanyon.com.*

Coffee and Quick Bites

Grab n' Go Coffee Shop

$ | **CAFÉ** | Located at Bright Angel Bicycles, next door to the Grand Canyon Visitor Center, this convenient coffee bar also serves fresh juices, sodas, and energy drinks as well as sandwiches, salads, and pastries. Everything is fresh and from Flagstaff favorites; the coffee beans are from Firehouse Coffee Company, the sandwiches and salads from Eat N' Run, and the bagels from Biff's Bagels. **Known for:** vegan and vegetarian options; items from popular Flagstaff eateries; trail-friendly foods. $ *Average main: $10* ⊠ *10 S. Entrance Rd., Grand Canyon National Park* ☎ *928/638–3055* ⊕ *bikegrandcanyon.com.*

Hotels

Bright Angel Lodge

$$ | **HOTEL** | Famed architect Mary Jane Colter designed this 1935 log-and-stone structure, which sits within a few yards of the canyon rim and blends superbly with the canyon walls; its location

is similar to El Tovar's but for about half the price. **Pros:** good value for the amazing location; charming rooms and cabins steps from the rim; on-site Internet kiosks and transportation desk for the mule ride. **Cons:** popular lobby is always packed; parking is a bit of a hike; only some rooms have canyon views. $ *Rooms from: $150* ⊠ *9 N. Village Loop Dr., Grand Canyon Village* ☎ *888/297–2757 reservations only, 928/638–2631* ⊕ *www.grandcanyonlodges.com* 🛏 *105 units* ⟋◯⟍ *No Meals.*

Lighten Your Load

Hikers staying at either Phantom Ranch or Bright Angel Campground can take advantage of the ranch's duffel service: bags or packs weighing 30 pounds or less can be transported to or from the ranch by mule for a fee of $83 each way. As is true for many desirable things at the canyon, reservations are a must. ☎ *303/297–2757* ⊕ *www.grandcanyonlodges.com.*

★ El Tovar Hotel

$$$$ | **HOTEL** | The hotel's European hunting-lodge atmosphere, attractively updated rooms and tile baths, and renowned dining room make it the best place to stay on the South Rim. A registered National Historic Landmark, the "architectural crown jewel of the Grand Canyon" was built in 1905 of Oregon pine logs and native stone. **Pros:** steps from the South Rim; fabulous lounge with outdoor seating and canyon views; best in-park dining. **Cons:** books up quickly; priciest lodging in the park; rooms are comfortable, not luxurious. $ *Rooms from: $400* ⊠ *1 El Tovar Rd., Grand Canyon Village* ☎ *888/297–2757 reservations only, 928/638–2631* ⊕ *www.grandcanyonlodges.com* 🛏 *78 rooms* ⟋◯⟍ *No Meals.*

Kachina Lodge

$$$$ | **HOTEL** | The well-appointed rooms at this motel-style lodge in Grand Canyon Village on the South Rim are a good bet for families and are within easy walking distance of dining facilities at nearby lodges. **Pros:** partial canyon views in half the rooms; family-friendly; steps from the best restaurants in the park. **Cons:** check-in at nearby El Tovar Hotel; limited parking; no air-conditioning. $ *Rooms from: $325* ⊠ *Desert View Dr., Grand Canyon Village* ☎ *888/297–2757 reservations only, 928/638–2631* ⊕ *www.grandcanyonlodges.com* 🛏 *47 rooms* ⟋◯⟍ *No Meals.*

Maswik Lodge

$$$$ | **HOTEL** | **FAMILY** | Far from the noisy crowds, Maswik accommodations are in two-story, contemporary motel-style buildings nestled in a shady ponderosa pine forest. **Pros:** units are modern,

spacious, and well equipped; good for families; affordable dining options. **Cons:** rooms lack historic charm; tucked away from the rim in the forest; no elevators to second floor of Maswik North. ⑤ *Rooms from: $320* ✉ *Grand Canyon Village* ☎ *888/297–2757 reservations only, 928/638–2631* ⊕ *www.grandcanyonlodges.com* ⇦ *280 rooms* ❍ *No Meals.*

Phantom Ranch

$ | **B&B/INN** | In a grove of cottonwood trees on the canyon floor, Phantom Ranch is accessible only to hikers, river rafters, and mule trekkers; there are 40 dormitory bunk beds and 14 beds in cabins, all with shared baths (though cabins have toilets and sinks). **Pros:** only inner-canyon lodging option; fabulous canyon views; remote access limits crowds. **Cons:** reservations are booked more than a year in advance; few amenities; shared bathrooms. ⑤ *Rooms from: $70* ✉ *On canyon floor, Grand Canyon National Park* ✛ *At intersection of Bright Angel and Kaibab trails* ☎ *303/297–2757, 888/297–2757* ⊕ *www.grandcanyonlodges.com* ⇦ *54 beds* ❍ *No Meals.*

Thunderbird Lodge

$$$$ | **HOTEL** | This motel with comfortable, simple rooms and partial canyon views has all the modern amenities you'd expect at a typical, midprice chain hotel—even pod coffeemakers. **Pros:** canyon views in some rooms; family-friendly; convenient to dining and activities in Grand Canyon Village. **Cons:** check-in at nearby Bright Angel Lodge; limited parking nearby; no air-conditioning (but some rooms have effective evaporative coolers). ⑤ *Rooms from: $325* ✉ *7 N. Village Loop Dr., Grand Canyon Village* ☎ *888/297–2757 reservations only, 928/638–2631* ⊕ *www.grandcanyonlodges.com* ⇦ *55 rooms* ❍ *No Meals.*

Yavapai Lodge

$$$$ | **HOTEL** | The largest motel-style lodge in the park is tucked in a piñon-pine and juniper forest at the eastern end of Grand Canyon Village, across from Market Plaza. **Pros:** transportation-activities desk in the lobby; walk to Market Plaza in Grand Canyon Village; only pet-friendly lodging at South Rim. **Cons:** farthest lodging in park from the rim (1 mile); generic appearance; no Wi-Fi in the rooms. ⑤ *Rooms from: $275* ✉ *11 Yavapai Lodge Rd., Grand Canyon Village* ☎ *877/404–4611 reservations only, 928/638–4001* ⊕ *www.visitgrandcanyon.com* ⇦ *358 rooms* ❍ *No Meals.*

Freebies at the Grand Canyon

While you're here, take advantage of the many complimentary services offered.

■ A system of free shuttle buses operates at the South Rim, catering to the road-weary, with four routes winding through or just outside the park. Two of these routes run year-round, including the Kaibab Rim Route which provides the only access to Yaki Point. Hikers coming or going from the South Kaibab Trailhead can also catch the Hikers' Express, which departs three times each morning from the Bright Angel Lodge, making a quick stop at the Backcountry Information Center before heading out to the South Kaibab Trailhead.

■ Free ranger-led programs are offered year-round, though more are scheduled during the busy spring and summer seasons. Programs include stargazing, geology, and the culture of prehistoric peoples. Some of the more in-depth programs may include a fossil walk or a condor talk, and there are seasonal programs including wildflower walks and fire ecology.

■ Kids ages four and older can get involved with the park's Junior Ranger program, with ever-changing activities including hikes and hands-on experiments.

■ Rangers will tell you that the best free activity in the canyon is watching the magnificent splashes of color on the canyon walls during sunrise and sunset.

🛍 Shopping

Nearly every lodging facility and retail store at the South Rim stocks arts and crafts made by Native American artists and Grand Canyon books and souvenirs. Prices are comparable to other souvenir outlets, though you may find some better deals in Williams. Nevertheless, a portion of the proceeds from items purchased at Kolb Studio, Tusayan Museum, and all the park visitor centers go to the nonprofit Grand Canyon Association.

Desert View Trading Post
SOUVENIRS | A mix of traditional Southwestern souvenirs and authentic Native American arts and crafts are for sale here. ⊠ *Desert View Dr., Grand Canyon National Park* ✛ *Near the Desert View Watchtower* ☎ *928/638–3150.*

Grand Canyon Conservancy Main Store

SOUVENIRS | Located at Visitor Center Plaza near the shuttle pickup and drop-off point, this store sells books, T-shirts, souvenirs, and national park-branded items. ⊠ *Mather Point, Grand Canyon National Park* ☎ *800/858–2808* ⊕ *www.grandcanyon.org.*

★ Hopi House

CRAFTS | This two-level shop near El Tovar and Verkamp's Visitor Center has the widest selection of Native American art and handicrafts in the vicinity. ⊠ *4 El Tovar Rd., Grand Canyon Village* ✣ *Across from El Tovar Hotel* ☎ *928/638–2631* ⊕ *www.grandcan-yonlodges.com.*

 Activities

BIKING

The South Rim's limited opportunities for off-road biking, narrow shoulders on park roads, and heavy traffic in summer may disappoint hard-core cyclists; for others, cycling is a fun and eco-friendly way to tour the park. Bicycles are permitted on all park roads and on the multiuse Greenway Trail System; visitors to the North Rim have Bridle Path and a 12-mile section of the Arizona Trail. Bikes are prohibited on the paved portions of the Rim Trail between Mather Point and Bright Angel Trailhead. Some find Hermit Road a good biking option, especially from March through November when it's closed to cars. You can ride west 8 miles and then put your bike on the free shuttle bus back into the village (or vice versa). A shorter ride takes you east to Yaki Point (3½ miles), a great place to stop and have a picnic. Bicyclists visiting the South Rim may also enjoy meandering through the ponderosa pine forest on the Greenway Trails or the Tusayan Bike Trail, a gentle uphill climb from Tusayan into the park. Rentals and guided bicycling tours are available mid-March through October at the South Rim from Bright Angel Bicycles (☎ *928/638–3055* ⊕ *bikegrandcanyon.com*) at the visitor center complex. Bicycle camping sites ($6 per person per night) are available at Mather Campground.

BOATING AND RAFTING

The National Park Service restricts the number of visitors allowed on the Colorado River each season, and seats fill up fast. Due to the limited availability, you should make reservations for multi-day trips at least a year and up to two in advance. June through August are the summer's peak period. If you're flexible, take advantage of the Arizona weather; May to early June and September are ideal rafting times in the Grand Canyon.

Most trips begin at Lees Ferry, a few miles below the Glen Canyon Dam near Page. Tranquil half- and full-day float trips make their way from the Glen Canyon Dam to Lees Ferry, but there are also raft trips that run from 3 to 18 days. (⇨ *For outfitters, see listings under Lees Ferry in the Gateways chapter.*) The shorter three- and four-day voyages either begin or end at Phantom Ranch at the bottom of the Grand Canyon at river mile 87. On the longer trips, you'll encounter the best of the canyon's white water along the way, including Lava Falls, listed in the *Guinness Book of World Records* as "the fastest navigable white water stretch in North America." Commercial outfitters provide life jackets, beverages, tents, sheets, tarps, sleeping bags, dry bags, first aid, and food— but you'll still need to pack clothing, a rain suit, hats, sunscreen, toiletries, and other sundries. On the river, you'll be allowed two waterproof bags to store items during the day. Keep in mind that one of the bags will be filled up with the provided sleeping bag and tarp, which leaves only one for your personal belongings.

CAMPING

Within the national park, there are two developed campgrounds on the South Rim and one on the North Rim. All campgrounds charge nightly camping fees; some accept reservations up to six months in advance (☎ 877/444–6777), while others are first-come, first-served.

Camping anywhere outside a developed rim campground, including in the canyon, requires a permit from the Backcountry Information Center, which also serves as your reservation. Permits can be requested by mail or fax only; applying well in advance is recommended. Call ☎ 928/638–7875 between 1 pm and 5 pm weekdays for information.

Bright Angel Campground. This backcountry campground is near Phantom Ranch at the bottom of the canyon. There are toilet facilities and running water but no showers. ⊠ *Intersection of South and North Kaibab trails, South Rim* ☎ *928/638–7875.*

Desert View Campground. Popular for spectacular views of the canyon from the nearby watchtower, this developed campground near the east entrance doesn't take reservations; show up before noon, as it fills up fast in summer. Open mid-May through mid-October, these sites have no hookups. ⊠ *Desert View Dr., 23 miles east of Grand Canyon Village off Hwy. 64, South Rim.*

Indian Garden. Halfway down the canyon is this campground, en route to Phantom Ranch on the Bright Angel Trail. Running water and toilet facilities are available, but not showers. A backcountry permit, which serves as a reservation, is required. You can book up to four months in advance. ⊠ *Bright Angel Trail* ☎ *928/638–7875, 928/638–2125.*

Mather Campground. The largest developed campground in the park is set in a forested area near Grand Canyon Village. Open all year, Mather takes reservations from March to November and has water and toilet facilities as well as showers and laundry (for an extra fee). There is a coffee bar/deli on-site, and the park shuttle stops here. ⊠ *Grand Canyon Village* ☎ *877/444–6777.*

Trailer Village. This campground in Grand Canyon Village has RV sites—but no tent-camping sites—with full hookups and bathroom facilities, though the bathrooms are ½ mile from the campground. The facility is very busy in spring and summer, so make reservations ahead of time. The dump station is closed in winter. ⊠ *Grand Canyon Village* ☎ *303/297–2757, 888/297–2757 reservations only, 303/297–3175 reservations only* ⊕ *www.visit-grandcanyon.com.*

CROSS-COUNTRY SKIING
Tusayan Ranger District
SKIING & SNOWBOARDING | Although you can't schuss down into the Grand Canyon, you can cross-country ski in the woods near the rim when there's enough snow, usually mid-December through early March. The ungroomed trails, suitable for beginner and intermediate skiers, begin at the Grandview Lookout and travel through the Kaibab National Forest. For details, contact the Tusayan Ranger District. ⊠ *176 Lincoln Log Loop, Grand Canyon* ☎ *928/220–5019* ⊕ *www.fs.usda.gov/kaibab.*

EDUCATIONAL PROGRAMS
Interpretive Ranger Programs. The National Park Service sponsors all sorts of orientation activities, such as daily guided hikes and talks, which change with the seasons. The focus may be on any aspect of the canyon—from geology and flora and fauna to history and early inhabitants. For schedules on the South Rim, go to any of the Grand Canyon visitor centers and pick up a free copy of the *Guide* or check online. ☎ *928/638–7888* ⊕ *www.nps.gov/grca* ▨ *Free.*

Junior Ranger Program. In summer, children ages four and up can take part in hands-on educational programs, including guided adventure hikes, ranger-led discovery talks, and book readings, and earn a Junior Ranger certificate and badge. Sign up at the Grand Canyon Conservancy Main Store in Visitor Center Plaza, Yavapai Geology Museum, or Kolb Studio. ☎ *928/638–7888* ⊕ *www.nps.gov/grca/forkids/beajuniorranger.htm* ▨ *Free.*

The challenging South Kaibab Trail descends from the trailhead at 7,260 feet down to 2,480 feet at the Colorado River.

FISHING

Anglers can hike into the canyon and cast a line in the Colorado River and its tributaries with a valid fishing license (required for residents and nonresidents ages 10 and up). Rainbow and brown trout, large and smallmouth bass, and catfish are common catches, but you can also hook sunfish, stripers, and walleye. Limits vary based on where you're fishing but are often generous; in fact, due to a trout reduction project in Bright Angel Creek, you are encouraged to keep as many rainbow and brown trout as you can catch in that creek's waters. No live bait is permitted.

HIKING

Although permits are not required for day hikes, you must have a backcountry permit for longer trips (⇨ *see Park Fees and Permits*). Some of the more popular trails are listed under Sights, including **Bright Angel Trail**, **Rim Trail**, and **South Kaibab Trail**; more detailed information and maps can be obtained from the Backcountry Information centers. Also, rangers can help design a trip to suit your abilities.

Remember that the canyon has significant elevation changes and, in summer, extreme temperature ranges, which can pose problems for people who aren't in good shape or who have heart or respiratory problems.

■ TIP→ **Carry plenty of water and energy foods.**

Listen to the podcast *Hike Smart* on the park's website to prepare for your trip. The majority of each year's 300-plus search-and-rescue incidents result from hikers underestimating the size of the canyon, hiking beyond their abilities, or not packing sufficient food and water.

■ TIP→ **Under no circumstances should you attempt a day hike from the rim to the river and back.**

Remember that when it's 85°F on the South Rim, it's 110°F on the canyon floor. Allow two to four days if you want to hike rim to rim (it's easier to descend from the North Rim,

Arranging Tours

Transportation-services desks are maintained at Bright Angel, Maswik Lodge, and Yavapai Lodge (closed in winter) in Grand Canyon Village. The desks provide information and handle bookings for sightseeing tours, taxi and bus services, and mule rides (but don't count on last-minute availability). There's also a concierge at El Tovar that can arrange most tours, with the exception of mule rides.

as it's more than 1,000 feet higher than the South Rim). Hiking steep trails from rim to rim is a strenuous trek of at least 21 miles and should be attempted only by experienced canyon hikers.

HORSEBACK RIDING

Private livestock is limited to the corridor trails (Bright Angel Trail and South Kaibab Trail) in the inner canyon and on select rim trails. Bright Angel and Cottonwood Campgrounds accommodate private equines, as does the South Rim Horse Camp, half a mile from the Bright Angel Trailhead. Grazing isn't permitted; handlers are required to pack their own feed. Backcountry permits are required for overnight horseback-riding trips and for overnight use of the South Rim Horse Camp.

Mule rides provide an intimate glimpse into the canyon for those who have the time, but not the stamina, to see the canyon on foot.

■ TIP→ **Reservations are essential and are accepted up to 13 months in advance.**

These trips have been conducted since the early 1900s. A comforting fact as you ride the narrow trail: no one has ever been killed while riding a mule that fell off a cliff. (Nevertheless, the treks are not for the faint of heart or people in questionable health.)

Did You Know?

Sure-footed mules take riders along the rim for half-day trips and down into the canyon for longer excursions. Two-day trips include an overnight stay at Phantom Ranch on the canyon floor.

★ Xanterra Parks & Resorts Mule Rides

HORSEBACK RIDING | These trips delve either into the canyon from the South Rim to Phantom Ranch, or east along the canyon's rim. Riders must be at least 9 years old and 57 inches tall, weigh less than 200 pounds for the Phantom Ranch ride or less than 225 pounds for the rim ride, and understand English. Children under 18 must be accompanied by an adult. Riders must be in fairly good physical condition, and pregnant women are advised not to take these trips.

The two-hour ride along the rim costs $170. An overnight mule ride with a stay in a cabin at Phantom Ranch at the bottom of the canyon, with meals included, is $1,165 ($2,110 for two riders). Package prices vary since a cabin at Phantom Ranch can accommodate up to four people. From November through March, you can stay for up to two nights at Phantom Ranch. Reservations are a must, but you can check at the Bright Angel Transportation Desk to see if there's last-minute availability. ⊠ *Grand Canyon Village* ☎ *888/297–2757, 303/297–2757* ⊕ *www.grandcanyonlodges.com.*

JEEP TOURS

Jeep rides can be rough; if you have had back injuries, check with your doctor before taking a 4x4 tour. It's a good idea to book a week or two ahead, and even longer if you're visiting in summer or on busy weekends.

Buck Wild Hummer Tours

DRIVING TOURS | With this tour company, you can see majestic rim views in Grand Canyon National Park and learn about the history, geology, and wildlife of the canyon from the comfort of a 13-passenger Hummer. Daily tours run either in the morning or at sunset. ⊠ *469 Hwy. 64, Grand Canyon* ☎ *928/362–5940* ⊕ *buckwildhummertours.com* 🎟 *From $104.*

Grand Canyon Jeep Tours & Safaris

FOUR-WHEELING | If you'd like to get off the pavement and see parts of the park that are accessible only by dirt road, a jeep tour can be just the ticket. From March through November, this tour operator leads daily three-hour off-road tours within the park, as well as jeep tours to a petroglyph site in Kaibab National Forest. Sunset tours to the canyon rim and combo tours adding helicopter or plane flights are also available. ⊠ *408 Hwy. 64, Tusayan* ☎ *928/638–5337* ⊕ *grandcanyonjeeptours.com* 🎟 *From $120.*

Pink Jeep Tours

FOUR-WHEELING | Ride in an open-air pink Jeep to some of the South Rim's best viewpoints. Some tours include short hikes or free IMAX tickets. ⊠ *450 Hwy. 64, Tusayan* ☎ *800/873–3662* ⊕ *www.pinkadventuretours.com* ✉ *From $109.*

SCENIC FLIGHTS

Flights by plane and helicopter over the canyon are offered by a number of companies, departing from the Grand Canyon Airport at the south end of Tusayan. Though the noise and disruption of so many aircraft buzzing around the canyon is controversial, "flight-seeing" remains a popular, if expensive, option. You'll have more visibility from a helicopter, but they're louder and more expensive.

Grand Canyon Airlines

ENTERTAINMENT CRUISE | This company offers a variety of plane tours, from a 45-minute fixed-wing tour of the eastern edge of the Grand Canyon, the North Rim, and the Kaibab Plateau to a half-day tour that combines flightseeing with a Hummer tour of the park. ⊠ *Grand Canyon Airport, Tusayan* ☎ *702/835–8484* ⊕ *www. grandcanyonairlines.com* ✉ *From $159.*

Maverick Helicopters

ENTERTAINMENT CRUISE | This company offers 25- and 45-minute tours of the South Rim, North Rim, and Dragon Corridor of the Grand Canyon, the widest and deepest part of the canyon. ⊠ *Grand Canyon Airport, Grand Canyon* ☎ *928/638–2622* ⊕ *www. maverickhelicopter.com* ✉ *From $319.*

Papillon Grand Canyon Helicopters

ENTERTAINMENT CRUISE | Leaving from Grand Canyon Airport, Papillon Grand Canyon Helicopters operates in tandem with Grand Canyon Airlines to offer fixed-wing plane and helicopter tours of the canyon. Add-on options include off-road jeep tours and smooth-water rafting trips. ⊠ *Grand Canyon Airport, Tusayan* ☎ *702/736–7243* ⊕ *www.papillon.com* ✉ *From $179 for fixed-wing plane; $239 for helicopter.*

Paragon Skydive

SKYDIVING | No experience is required to tandem skydive from 16,000 feet to the highest drop zone in the world at the canyon's rim. As you descend, take in the Grand Canyon with no engine noise to distract you. Packages start at $329. ⊠ *Grand Canyon National Park Airport* ☎ *928/224–9661* ⊕ *skydivegc.com.*

Westwind Air Service

ENTERTAINMENT CRUISE | This fixed-wing, narrated plane tour soars over the widest and deepest part of the canyon as well as the North Rim and Kaibab National Forest. There's a two-passenger minimum. ⊠ *Grand Canyon National Park Airport* ☏ *480/991–5557, 888/869–50866* ⊕ *www.westwindairservice.com*.

THE NORTH RIM

Updated by
Teresa Bitler

⛰ Camping	🛏 Hotels	🏃 Activities	👁 Scenery	👥 Crowds
★☆☆☆☆	★☆☆☆☆	★★☆☆☆	★★★★★	★☆☆☆☆

WELCOME TO THE NORTH RIM

TOP REASONS TO GO

★ **Less crowded:** Because it requires more effort to visit, the North Rim does not draw the crowds the South Rim does. It's a quieter and more peaceful experience.

★ **More beautiful:** Some argue that the views at the North Rim are even more breathtaking than those at the South Rim. Either way, the North Rim offers a different perspective on the canyon.

★ **Cooler:** On average, it's nearly 10 degrees Fahrenheit cooler at the North Rim than it is at the South Rim, making it more comfortable during the summer.

★ **Activities:** Since there are fewer visitors, you'll have a better chance of booking a mule ride at the North Rim. Guided hikes and ranger-led programs have fewer participants, too.

★ **Wildlife:** In addition to more common species, the rare Kaibab squirrel is found only on the North Rim, and the once nearly extinct California condor now soars over canyon walls here.

A 4½-hour drive from the South Rim of Grand Canyon National Park, the North Rim is much smaller in scale than its cross-the-canyon counterpart. A scenic drive links Point Imperial to Cape Royal. The only way to access the North Rim by car is via Highway 67. Due to weather, the North Rim and Highway 67 are open only from May 15 through Oct. 15.

1 Bright Angel Point. The most popular viewpoint on the North Rim and a short walk from Grand Canyon Lodge, Bright Angel Point offers a look into Bright Angel Canyon and into the main canyon.

2 Point Imperial. At over 8,800 feet, Point Imperial is the highest in Grand Canyon National Park and sits at its northernmost boundary. From here, you can see where the narrow walls of Marble Canyon open into the park's chasm.

3 Cape Royal. The last stop on the scenic drive from the North Rim's visitor center, Cape Royal provides panoramic views from Marble Canyon in the east and across the canyon to Mather Point.

4 Walhalla Glades. These Puebloan ruins housed farming families from about 1050 to 1150 AD. More than 100 farm sites have been found on the Walhalla Plateau.

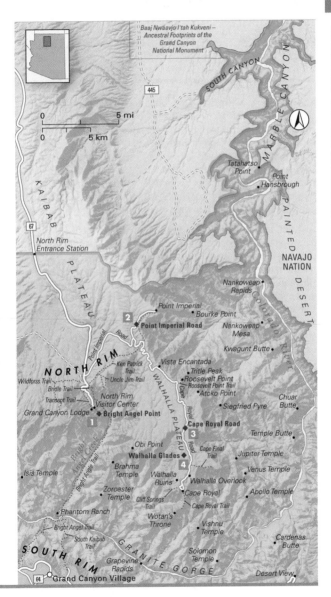

Baaj Nwaavjo I'tah Kukveni –
Ancestral Footprints of the
Grand Canyon
National Monument

SOUTH CANYON

MARBLE CANYON

445

0   5 mi
0   5 km

K A I B A B

67

North Rim
Entrance Station

Tatahatso
Point

Point
Hansbrough

P A I N T E D

PLATEAU

NAVAJO
NATION

Nankoweap
Rapids

Point Imperial

2   Point Imperial Road

Bourke Point

Nankoweap
Mesa

Colorado River

D E S E R T

Point Imperial Road

N O R T H   R I M

Ken Patrick
Trail

Wildforss Trail

Bridle Trail

Transept Trail

North Rim
Visitor Center

1   Bright Angel Point

Grand Canyon Lodge

Uncle Jim Trail

Vista Encantada

Tritle Peak

Roosevelt Point

Roosevelt Point Trail

Atoko Point

Kwagunt Butte

Siegfried Pyre

Chuar
Butte

WALHALLA PLATEAU

Cape Royal Road

3   Cape Royal Road

Temple Butte

Royal Road

Bright Angel Creek

Obi Point

Walhalla Glades

4

Cape Final
Trail

Jupiter Temple

Isis Temple

Brahma
Temple

Walhalla
Ruins

Venus Temple

Zoroaster
Temple

Cliff Springs
Trail

Walhalla Overlook

Cape Royal

Cape Royal Trail

Apollo Temple

Bright Angel Trail

Phantom Ranch

Wotan's
Throne

Vishnu
Temple

Bright Angel Trail

South Kaibab
Trail

G R A N I T E   G O R G E

Solomon
Temple

Cardenas
Butte

S O U T H   R I M

Grapevine
Rapids

64   Grand Canyon Village

Desert View

Author Edward Abbey once wrote: "I find that in contemplating the natural world my pleasure is greater if there are not too many others contemplating it with me, at the same time."

The North Rim will give you that opportunity. Although it draws only about 10% of the Grand Canyon's visitors, many believe it is more gorgeous than the South Rim, and because of its remote location, it provides a more intimate and unhurried experience. Although the North Rim is just 10 miles across from the South Rim, getting there by car is a 4½-hour, 215-mile drive. At first it might not sound like the trip would be worth it, but the payoff is huge: those who make the North Rim trip often insist it has the canyon's most beautiful views and best hiking.

At 1,000 feet higher than the South Rim, the northern edge offers more expansive vistas of the buttes and ridges scattered through the wide expanse cut by the Colorado River millions of years ago. It's these long distances and lack of amenities that keep the North Rim and the surrounding Kaibab National Forest a pristine wonderland perfect for outdoor enthusiasts looking to explore shaded forests, broad meadows, and hidden waterways. The Paiute word Kaibab means "mountain lying down," and this 9,000-foot-tall limestone plateau is just that—one of the highest points on the vast Colorado Plateau. The road to these alpine uplands rises out of the surrounding desert to an isolated forest stretching along the upper reaches of the Grand Canyon. Wildlife abounds in the thick ponderosa pine forests and lush mountain meadows. It's common to see deer, turkeys, and coyotes as you drive through this remote region.

Planning

When to Go

The North Rim is open May 15 through October 15. The rest of the year, the North Rim and Highway 67 leading into it are closed due to the snow this area receives. If you visit the first or last month of the season, expect temperatures to hover around 60 degrees

Fahrenheit during the day and dip below freezing at night. The trade-off, though, is you'll have better luck finding accommodations at the lodge or booking a mule trip then. Although the North Rim never gets crowded the way the South Rim does, it does see more visitors in July and August when temperatures average in the mid-70s. Monsoon storms are common during the summer months, and the aspens in the park change color in the fall.

Getting Here and Around

AIR
There are two airports equidistant from the North Rim. The first is Page Municipal Airport, approximately 150 miles away in Page, Arizona. You can fly directly from Phoenix Sky Harbor International Airport to Page on Contour Airlines and rent a car at the airport. It's roughly a two-hour drive from Page to the North Rim. Also about 150 miles away, St. George Regional Airport is serviced by United Airlines, American Airlines, and Delta Airlines. Another option is flying into Harry Reid International Airport in Las Vegas, roughly 275 miles from the North Rim, or Phoenix Sky Harbor, 350 miles away.

CAR
A car is essential not only to get to the North Rim but to explore it. Visitors coming from south of the Grand Canyon can pick up Highway 89 in Flagstaff and continue to Highway 89A. Take Highway 89A to Jacob Lake at its intersection with Highway 67. Turn left onto Highway 67 and follow it into the park. From Page, head south on Highway 89 to Highway 89A, and follow Highway 89A to Highway 67 and on to the park's entrance. From Las Vegas, go north on Interstate 15 to St. George. Turn right on Highway 9, picking up Highway 59 before leaving St. George. Highway 59 becomes Highway 389 in Colorado City. Continue to Fredonia where the highway ends at Highway 89A. Turn right, and drive 30 miles to Highway 67. Turn right again to enter the park. Inside the park, there is no shuttle service transporting visitors from one scenic overlook to the next. You will need a car to visit the outlying viewpoints.

SHUTTLE
The North Rim does have a Hiker Shuttle that transports hikers from the Grand Canyon Lodge to the North Kaibab Trailhead at 5:45 am and 7:10 am every day. You must make reservations 24 hours in advance at the lodge to guarantee a spot. While there isn't a shuttle to take visitors from one viewpoint to the next,

there is a shuttle that takes hikers from the North Rim to the South Rim and vice versa. This is mainly for rim-to-rim hikers who left their vehicle on the South Rim when they descended into the canyon.

Hotels

There is only one hotel, the Grand Canyon Lodge, on the North Rim of Grand Canyon National Park. If you want to stay in the park, make reservations for the historic lodge's rooms and cabins at least six months in advance. A campground is about a mile from the lodge. Just 5 miles from the park's entrance, Kaibab Lodge offers the closest option outside the park. Jacob Lake Inn and the neighboring campground, Jacob Lake Recreational Area, are located at the intersection of Highway 67 and Highway 89A. You'll find motels on Highway 89A between Marble Canyon and Jacob Lake and chain hotels in Kanab, Utah, 80 miles from the North Rim. There are more chain options 120 miles away in Page, Arizona.

Restaurants

For a sit-down, order-off-a-menu meal, you have only one option at the North Rim, the main restaurant at the Grand Canyon Lodge. There's also a deli, coffee shop, and saloon in the national park. The motels and lodges on U.S. Highway 89A have small restaurants but aren't practical unless you're coming to or leaving the park. For variety, chain restaurants, or fast food, you'll have to drive two hours to Page, Arizona, something that isn't practical while staying in the park.

⇨ *Hotel prices in the reviews are the lowest cost of a standard double room in high season. Restaurant prices in the reviews are the average cost of a main course at dinner, or if dinner is not served, at lunch.*

What It Costs in U.S. Dollars			
$	$$	$$$	$$$$
HOTELS			
under $120	$120–$175	$176–$250	over $250
RESTAURANTS			
under $12	$12–$20	$21–$30	over $30

Perched on the North Rim's edge—1,000 feet higher than the South Rim—is the Grand Canyon Lodge.

Tours

The national park hosts free daily ranger programs on the North Rim. Programs range from geology and fossils to plants, animals, and people. These can include walks, talks, hikes, and demonstrations. Several evening programs are held, too, including the annual Star Party event every June, featuring telescopes, constellation talks, and more.

The North Rim

Sights

PICNIC AREAS

Cape Royal, 23 miles south of the North Rim Visitor Center, at the end of Cape Royal Road, is the most popular designated picnic area on the North Rim due to its panoramic views. **Point Imperial,** 11 miles northeast of the North Rim Visitor Center, has shade and some privacy.

SCENIC DRIVES

★ Highway 67

SCENIC DRIVE | Open mid-May to roughly mid-October (or the first big snowfall), this two-lane paved road climbs 1,400 feet in elevation as it passes through the Kaibab National Forest. Also

Brighty of the Grand Canyon

Cast in bronze, the life-sized statue of a burro sits in the Grand Canyon Lodge sunroom, gazing out at the Grand Canyon through a wall of windows. The statue is modeled after a real-life burro named Brighty, who played a role in Grand Canyon history and roamed the canyon from around 1892 until 1922. Famous children's author Marguerite Henry chronicled this wild burro's life in the book *Brighty of the Grand Canyon* in 1953. While you're here, you might notice that the statue's nose is shiny where countless visitors have rubbed it for good luck.

called the North Rim Parkway, this scenic route crosses the limestone-capped Kaibab Plateau—passing broad meadows, sun-dappled forests, and small lakes and springs—before abruptly falling away at the abyss of the Grand Canyon. Wildlife abounds in the thick ponderosa pine forests and lush mountain meadows. It's common to see deer, turkeys, and coyotes as you drive through such a remote region. Point Imperial and Cape Royal branch off this scenic drive, which runs from Jacob Lake to Bright Angel Point. ⊠ *Hwy. 67, Grand Canyon National Park.*

HISTORIC SIGHTS
Grand Canyon Lodge
HOTEL | Built in 1936 by the Union Pacific Railroad (replacing the original 1928 building, which burned in a fire), this massive stone structure is listed on the National Register of Historic Places. Its huge sunroom has hardwood floors, high-beamed ceilings, and a marvelous view of the canyon through plate-glass windows. On warm days, visitors sit in the sun and drink in the surrounding beauty on an outdoor viewing deck, where National Park Service employees deliver free lectures on geology and history. The dining room serves breakfast, lunch, and dinner; the Roughrider Saloon is a bar by night and a coffee shop in the morning. ⊠ *Grand Canyon National Park* ✛ *Off Hwy. 67 near Bright Angel Point* ☎ *928/638–7888 May.–Oct., 877/386–4383 reservations* ⊕ *www. grandcanyonnorth.com* ☉ *Closed mid-Oct.–mid-May.*

SCENIC STOPS
★ Bright Angel Point
VIEWPOINT | Bright Angel Point is one of the most awe-inspiring overlooks on either rim. To get to it, follow the trail that starts on the grounds of the Grand Canyon Lodge and runs along the crest of a point of rocks that juts into the canyon for several hundred

Grand Canyon
North Rim

↑ TO
JACOB LAKE, MARBLE CANYON,
AND SOUTH RIM

Baaj Nwaavjo I'tah Kukveni –Ancestral
Footprints of the Grand Canyon
National Monument

SOUTH CANYON

MARBLE CANYON

445

KEY

🏕 Ranger Station
🔺 Campground
🍴 Picnic Area
🍴 Restaurant
🏞 Lodge
- - - Trails
= = = Dirt Roads

0   5 mi

0   5 km

Tatahatso
Point

Point
Hansbrough

KAIBAB

North Rim
Entrance Station

PAINTED

NAVAJO
NATION

Highway 67

67

PLATEAU

Nankoweap
Rapids

Colorado River

DESERT

• Point Sublime

Point Imperial

🍴 Point Imperial

• Bourke Point

Nankoweap
Mesa

Point Imperial Road

Kwagunt Butte

NORTH RIM

Vista Encantada

Tittle Peak

Ken Patrick Trail

Wildforss Trail

Uncle Jim Trail

Bridle
Trail

North Kaibab
Trailhead

North Rim
Visitor Center

Transept Trail

Grand Canyon Lodge

Bright Angel Point

Cottonwood
Campground

WALHALLA PLATEAU

Roosevelt Point

Roosevelt Point Trail

Cape

• Atoko Point

Royal

Siegfried Pyre

Chuar
Butte

Temple Butte

Obi Point

Walhalla Glades

Road

• Brahma
Temple

Walhalla
Ruins

Cape Final
Trail

Walhalla Overlook

Jupiter Temple

Venus Temple

Isis Temple

Bright Angel Trail

North Kaibab Trail

• Zoroaster
Temple

Cliff Spring
Trail

Cape Royal

Apollo Temple

Horn Creek
Rapids

Phantom Ranch

Cape Royal
Trail

Wotan's
Throne

Vishnu
Temple

Cardenas
Butte

PALISADES OF THE DESERT

SOUTH RIM

Mather
Point

Yaki Point

Grapevine
Rapids

GRANITE GORGE

Hance Rapids

Solomon
Temple

Desert View

64

Grand Canyon Village

Navajo Point

yards. The walk is only ½ mile round-trip, but it's an exciting trek accented by sheer drops on each side of the trail. In a few spots where the route is extremely narrow, metal railings ensure visitors' safety. The temptation to clamber out on precarious perches to have your picture taken should be resisted at all costs. ⊠ *North Rim Dr., Grand Canyon National Park* ✛ *Near Grand Canyon Lodge.*

Cape Royal

TRAIL | A popular sunset destination, Cape Royal showcases the canyon's jagged landscape; you'll also get a glimpse of the Colorado River, framed by a natural stone arch called Angels Window. In autumn, the aspens turn a beautiful gold, adding even more color to an already magnificent scene of the forested surroundings. The easy and rewarding 1-mile round-trip hike along Cliff Springs Trail starts here; it takes you through a forested ravine and terminates at Cliff Springs, where the forest opens to another impressive view of the canyon walls. ⊠ *Cape Royal Scenic Dr., Grand Canyon National Park* ✛ *23 miles southeast of Grand Canyon Lodge.*

Point Imperial

VIEWPOINT | At 8,803 feet, Point Imperial has the highest vista point at either rim. It offers magnificent views of both the canyon and the distant country: the Vermilion Cliffs to the north, the 10,000-foot Navajo Mountain to the northeast in Utah, the Painted Desert to the east, and the Little Colorado River canyon to the southeast. Other prominent points of interest include views of Mt. Hayden, Saddle Mountain, and Marble Canyon. ⊠ *Point Imperial Rd., Grand Canyon National Park* ✛ *11 miles northeast of Grand Canyon Lodge.*

★ Point Sublime

VIEWPOINT | You can camp within feet of the canyon's edge at this awe-inspiring site. Sunrises and sunsets are spectacular. The winding road, through gorgeous high country, is only 17 miles, but it will take you at least two hours one-way. The road is intended only for vehicles with high road clearance (pickups and four-wheel-drive vehicles). It is also necessary to be properly equipped for wilderness road travel. Check with a park ranger or at the information desk at Grand Canyon Lodge before taking this journey. You may camp here only with a permit from the Backcountry Information Center. ⊠ *North Rim Dr., Grand Canyon National Park* ✛ *About 20 miles west of North Rim Visitor Center.*

En Route

As you journey to the North Rim from Lees Ferry, the immense blue-green bulk of the Kaibab Plateau stretches out before you. About 18 miles past Navajo Bridge, a sign directs you to the **San Bartolome Historic Site**, an overlook with plaques that tell the story of the Dominguez-Escalante expedition of 1776. At **House Rock Valley**, a large road sign announces the House Rock Buffalo Ranch, operated by the Arizona Game and Fish Department. A 23-mile dirt road leads to the home of one of the largest herds of American bison in the Southwest. You may drive out to the ranch, but be aware that you may not see any buffalo—the expanse of their range is so great that they frequently cannot be spotted from a car.

Roosevelt Point

VIEWPOINT | Named after the president who gave the Grand Canyon its national monument status in 1908 (it was upgraded to national park status in 1919), Roosevelt Point is the best place to see the confluence of the Little Colorado River and the Grand Canyon. The cliffs above the Colorado River south of the junction are known as the Palisades of the Desert. A short woodland loop trail leads to this eastern viewpoint. ⊠ *Cape Royal Rd., Grand Canyon National Park* ✤ *18 miles east of Grand Canyon Lodge.*

Vista Encantada

VIEWPOINT | This point on the Walhalla Plateau offers views of the upper drainage of Nankoweap Creek, a rock pinnacle known as Brady Peak, and the Painted Desert to the east. This is an enchanting place for a picnic lunch. ⊠ *Cape Royal Rd., Grand Canyon National Park* ✤ *16 miles southeast of Grand Canyon Lodge.*

Walhalla Overlook

VIEWPOINT | One of the lowest elevations on the North Rim, this overlook has views of the Unkar Delta, a fertile region used by Ancestral Pueblo as farmland. These ancient people also gathered food and hunted game on the North Rim. A flat path leads to the remains of the Walhalla Glades Pueblo, which was inhabited from 1050 to 1150 AD. ⊠ *Cape Royal Rd., Grand Canyon National Park* ✤ *22½ miles southeast of Grand Canyon Lodge.*

Flora and Fauna

Ninety-one mammal species inhabit Grand Canyon National Park, as well as 447 species of birds, 58 kinds of reptiles and amphibians, and 17 kinds of fish. The rare Kaibab squirrel is found only on the North Rim—you can recognize it by its all-white tail and black underside. The pink Grand Canyon rattlesnake lives at lower elevations within the canyon. Hawks and ravens are visible year-round. The endangered California condor has been reintroduced to the canyon region. Park rangers give daily talks on the magnificent birds, whose wingspan measures nine feet. In spring, summer, and fall, mule deer (recognizable by their large ears) and elk are abundant at the South Rim. Don't be fooled by gentle appearances; these guys can be aggressive. It's illegal to feed them, as it'll disrupt their natural habitats and increase your risk of getting bitten or kicked.

The best times to see wildlife are early in the morning and late in the afternoon. Look for out-of-place shapes and motions, keeping in mind that animals occupy all layers in a natural habitat and not just at your eye level.

More than 1,700 species of plants color the park. The South Rim's Coconino Plateau is fairly flat and covered with stands of piñon and ponderosa pines, junipers, and Gambel's oak trees. On the North Rim's Kaibab Plateau, Douglas fir, spruce, and quaking aspen prevail. In spring you're likely to see asters, sunflowers, and lupine in bloom at both rims.

TRAILS

Cape Final Trail

TRAIL | This 4-mile round-trip gravel path follows an old jeep trail through a ponderosa pine forest to the canyon overlook at Cape Final with panoramic views of the northern canyon, the Palisades of the Desert, and the impressive spectacle of Juno Temple. *Easy.* ⊠ *Grand Canyon National Park* ⊹ *Trailhead: dirt parking lot 5 miles south of Roosevelt Point on Cape Royal Rd.*

Cape Royal Trail

TRAIL | **FAMILY** | Informative signs about vegetation, wildlife, and natural history add to this popular 0.8-mile, round-trip, paved path to Cape Royal; allow at least one hour round-trip. At an elevation of 7,685 feet on the southern edge of the Walhalla Plateau, this popular viewpoint offers expansive views of Wotans Throne, Vishnu Temple, Freya Castle, Horseshoe Mesa, and the Colorado

Off the Path

Unpaved forested side roads branch off Highway 67 before the North Rim park entrance station, leading to several remote viewpoints not seen by the majority of Grand Canyon travelers. At Crazy Jug Point, you'll see the Colorado River as well as several canyon landmarks, including Powell Plateau, Great Thumb Mesa, and Tapeats Amphitheater. Timp Point features spectacular canyon views and a glimpse of Thunder River. Check with the Kaibab Forest Visitors Center in Jacob Lake for maps and road updates. The U.S. Forest Service maintains everything north of the rim, which is monitored by the National Park Service.

River. The trail also offers several nice views of Angels Window. *Easy.* ⊠ *Grand Canyon National Park* ✛ *Trailhead: end of Cape Royal Rd.*

Cliff Spring Trail

TRAIL | An easy 1-mile (round-trip), one-hour walk near Cape Royal, Cliff Spring Trail leads through a forested ravine to an excellent view of the canyon. The trailhead begins at the Cape Royal parking lot, across from Angels Window Overlook. Narrow and precarious in spots, it passes ancient dwellings, winds beneath a limestone overhang, and ends at Cliff Springs. (Do not drink the water.) *Easy.* ⊠ *Grand Canyon National Park* ✛ *Trailhead: end of Cape Royal Rd.*

Ken Patrick Trail

TRAIL | This primitive trail, one of the longest on the North Rim, travels 10 miles one-way (allow six hours each way) from the trailhead at 8,250 feet to Point Imperial at 8,803 feet. It crosses drainages and occasionally detours around fallen trees. The end of the road, at Point Imperial, brings the highest views from either rim. Note that there is no water along this trail. *Difficult.* ⊠ *Grand Canyon National Park* ✛ *Trailhead: east side of North Kaibab trailhead parking lot.*

North Kaibab Trail

TRAIL | At 8,241 feet, this trail leads into the canyon and down to Phantom Ranch. It is recommended for experienced hikers only, who should allow four days for the round-trip hike. The long, steep path drops 5,840 feet over a distance of 14½ miles to Phantom Ranch and the Colorado River, so the National Park Service suggests that day hikers not go farther than Roaring Springs (5,020 feet) before turning to hike back up out of the canyon. After about 7 miles, Cottonwood Campground (4,080 feet) has drinking water in summer, restrooms, shade trees, and a ranger. ■ TIP→ **A free shuttle takes hikers to the North Kaibab trailhead twice daily from Grand Canyon Lodge; reserve a spot the day before.** *Difficult.* ⊠ *Grand Canyon National Park ⊹ Trailhead: about 2 miles north of Grand Canyon Lodge.*

Roosevelt Point Trail

TRAIL | FAMILY | This easy 0.2-mile round-trip trail loops through the forest to the scenic viewpoint. Allow 20 minutes for this relaxed, secluded hike. *Easy.* ⊠ *Grand Canyon National Park ⊹ Trailhead: Cape Royal Rd.*

Transept Trail

TRAIL | FAMILY | This 3-mile round-trip, 1½-hour trail begins near the Grand Canyon Lodge at 8,255 feet. Well maintained and well marked, it has little elevation change, sticking near the rim before reaching a dramatic view of a large stream through Bright Angel Canyon. The trail leads to Transept Canyon, which geologist Clarence Dutton named in 1882, declaring it "far grander than Yosemite." Check the posted schedule to find a ranger talk along this trail; it's also a great place to view fall foliage. Flash floods can occur any time of the year, especially June through September when thunderstorms develop rapidly. *Easy.* ⊠ *Grand Canyon National Park ⊹ Trailhead: near Grand Canyon Lodge east patio.*

Uncle Jim Trail

TRAIL | This 5-mile, three-hour loop starts at 8,300 feet and winds south through the forest, past Roaring Springs and Bright Angel canyons. The highlight of this rim hike is Uncle Jim Point, which, at 8,244 feet, overlooks the upper sections of the North Kaibab Trail. *Moderate.* ⊠ *Grand Canyon National Park ⊹ Trailhead: North Kaibab Trail parking lot.*

Widforss Trail

TRAIL | Round-trip, Widforss Trail is 9.6 miles, with an elevation change of only 200 feet. Allow five to six hours for the hike, which starts at 8,080 feet and passes through shady forests of pine, spruce, fir, and aspen on its way to Widforss Point, at 7,900 feet. Here you'll have good views of five temples: Zoroaster, Brahma, and Deva to the southeast, and Buddha and Manu to the southwest. You are likely to see wildflowers in summer, and this is a good trail for viewing fall foliage. It's named in honor of artist Gunnar M. Widforss, renowned for his paintings of national park landscapes. *Moderate.* ⊠ *Grand Canyon National Park ⊹ Trailhead: off dirt road about 2 miles north of Grand Canyon Lodge.*

VISITOR CENTERS

North Rim Visitor Center

VISITOR CENTER | View exhibits, peruse the bookstore, and pick up useful maps and brochures at this visitor center. Interpretive programs are often scheduled in summer. If you're craving refreshments, it's a short walk from here to the Roughrider Saloon at the Grand Canyon Lodge. ⊠ *Near Grand Canyon Lodge at North Rim, Grand Canyon National Park* ☎ *928/638–7864* ⊕ *www.nps.gov/grca.*

 Restaurants

★ Grand Canyon Lodge Dining Room

$$$ | **SOUTHWESTERN** | The high wood-beamed ceilings, stone walls, and spectacular views in this spacious, historic room are perhaps the biggest draw for the lodge's main restaurant. Dinner includes southwestern steak-house fare that would make any cowboy feel at home, including selections such as bison and venison. **Known for:** incredible views; charming, historic room; steaks, fish, game, and vegetarian selections. ⑤ *Average main: $30* ⊠ *Grand Canyon Lodge, Bright Angel Point, North Rim* ☎ *928/638–2611* ⊕ *www.grandcanyonnorth.com* ☉ *Closed mid-Oct.–mid-May.*

☕ Coffee and Quick Bites

The Coffee Shop

$ | **AMERICAN** | From 5:30 to 10:30 am, the Roughrider Saloon operates as a coffee shop serving pastries, breakfast burritos, and grab-and-go fare. Seating is limited, but you can watch the sunrise as you sip your coffee on the deck. **Known for:** best place to get your caffeine fix; quick breakfasts to go; coffee served at a saloon bar. ⑤ *Average main: $10* ⊠ *Grand Canyon Lodge, North Rim* ☎ *928/638–2611* ⊕ *www.grandcanyonforever.com.*

Deli in the Pines

$ | **AMERICAN** | Dining choices are limited on the North Rim, but this deli next to the lodge is your best bet for a meal on a budget or grabbing a premade sandwich on the go. Selections also include pizza (gluten-free or standard crust), salads, custom-made sandwiches, and soft-serve ice cream. **Known for:** convenient quick bite; sandwiches to take on the trail; outdoor seating. ⑤ *Average main: $12* ⊠ *Grand Canyon Lodge, Bright Angel Point, North Rim* ☎ *928/638–2611* ⊕ *www.grandcanyonnorth.com* ☉ *Closed mid-Oct.–mid-May.*

Hotels

★ Grand Canyon Lodge

$$$ | HOTEL | This historic property, constructed mainly in the 1920s and '30s, is the only lodging on the North Rim. The main building has locally quarried limestone walls and timbered ceilings. **Pros:** steps away from gorgeous North Rim views; close to several easy hiking trails; historic lodge building is a national landmark. **Cons:** fills up fast; limited amenities; most cabins far from main lodge building. ⑤ *Rooms from: $180* ⊠ *Hwy. 67, North Rim* ☎ *877/386–4383 reservations, 928/638–2611 May–Oct.* ⊕ *www. grandcanyonnorth.com* ⊗ *Closed mid-Oct.–mid-May* ⇆ *219 rooms* ⦿ *No Meals.*

Shopping

General Store

GENERAL STORE | Located next to the campground, this rustic store sells basic groceries, camping supplies, and souvenirs. There's also an ATM and gas station on-site. ⊠ *North Rim, North Rim* ⊹ *Hwy. 67* ☎ *928/638–2611* ⊗ *Closed mid-Oct.–mid-May.*

Grand Canyon Lodge Gift Shop

SOUVENIRS | Authentic Navajo rugs, colorful kachina, carvings, and other Native American crafts share space with national park souvenirs, T-shirts, and books at this gift shop in Grand Canyon Lodge. ⊠ *Grand Canyon Lodge, North Rim* ☎ *928/638–2611* ⊕ *www. grandcanyonforever.com* ⊗ *Closed mid-Oct.–mid-May.*

Activities

BIKING

Mountain bikers can test the many dirt access roads found in this remote area. The 17-mile trek to Point Sublime is, well, sublime; though you'll share this road with high-clearance vehicles, it's rare to spot other people on most of these primitive pathways.

Bicycles and leashed pets are allowed on the well-maintained 1.2-mile (one-way) **Bridle Trail,** which follows the road from Grand Canyon Lodge to the North Kaibab Trailhead. A 12-mile section of the **Arizona Trail** is also open to bicycles; it passes through pine forests within the park and continues north into Kaibab National Forest. Bikes are prohibited on all other national park trails.

Winter Activities

Due to heavy snows and extreme winter weather, the North Rim closes all its services from mid-October through mid-May. Highway 67, however, stays open to the North Rim until snows force the closure of the road at Jacob Lake, usually mid- to late November. After the road closes, the rim can be accessed by hiking, snowshoeing, and cross-country skiing. Winter visitors must obtain a backcountry permit for overnight use during the winter season (mid-October through mid-May). Between the North Kaibab trailhead and Bright Angel Point, all overnight visitors are required to stay at the North Rim Campground. Winter campers can camp at large at all other areas between the northern boundary and the North Kaibab trailhead.

CAMPING

North Rim Campground. The only designated campground at the North Rim of Grand Canyon National Park sits in a pine forest 3 miles north of the rim and has 84 RV and tent sites (no hookups). Reserve in advance. ✉ *Hwy. 67, North Rim* ☎ *877/444–6777* ⊕ *www.recreation.gov.*

EDUCATIONAL PROGRAMS

Interpretive Ranger Programs

ECOTOURISM | Grand Canyon National Park holds ranger-led talks and hikes Thursday through Sunday. Topics range from geology talks and critter chats to fossil walks and family-friendly activities. Some evening programs, such as star gazing, are also available. ✉ *Grand Canyon National Park* ☎ *928/638–7967* ⊕ *www.nps.gov/grca.*

Junior Ranger Program

ECOTOURISM | FAMILY | Children ages four and up can be sworn in as junior rangers at the South Rim after completing designated tasks, including attending a ranger-led program, drawing the canyon, and writing a poem. Similarly, those that hike or ride a mule to the canyon's bottom, regardless of age, can earn a Grand Canyon Explorer Junior Ranger merit badge. Pick up a South Rim activity book at the Grand Canyon Conservancy Main Store, Yavapai Geology Museum, or Kolb Studio. You can pick up the guide for the Grand Canyon Explorer program at corridor trail campgrounds or backcountry ranger stations. ✉ *Grand Canyon National Park* ☎ *928/638–7967* ⊕ *www.nps.gov/grca.*

HIKING

Because much of the North Rim sits at an elevation between 8,000 and 9,000 feet, hiking on the North Rim can be more taxing than what you're used to back home. Fortunately, several of the above-rim trails are ½-mile or less and lead to scenic viewpoints. More physically fit hikers can tackle the park's longer hikes, including the North Kaibab Trail, the only trail that descends to the canyon floor from the North Rim. Leashed pets are allowed only on the Bridle Path and Arizona Trail with the exception of service animals, which must be checked in with the Backcountry Information Center before heading out on the trails.

HORSEBACK RIDING

Private livestock is limited to the corridor trail (North Kaibab Trail) in the inner canyon and on select rim trails including Uncle Jim Trail. Bright Angel and Cottonwood Campgrounds accommodate private equines as does the North Rim Horse Camp, ¼ mile from the North Kaibab Trailhead. Grazing isn't permitted; handlers are required to pack their own feed. A backcountry permit is required for any overnight use of private stock.

Canyon Trail Rides

HORSEBACK RIDING | FAMILY | This company leads mule rides along the easier trails of the North Rim. Options include one- and three-hour rides along the rim or a three-hour ride down into the canyon (minimum age seven for one-hour rides, 10 for three-hour rides). Weight limits are 200 pounds for canyon rides and 220 pounds for the rim rides. Available daily from May 15 to October 15, these excursions are popular, so make reservations in advance. ✉ *North Rim* ☎ *435/679–8665* ⊕ *www.canyonrides.com* 🖾 *$50 for one-hour ride; $100 for three-hour.*

THE WEST RIM AND HAVASU CANYON

Updated by
Teresa Bitler

🏕 Camping	🛏 Hotels	🏃 Activities	👁 Scenery	🚻 Crowds
★★☆☆☆	★★☆☆☆	★★★☆☆	★★★★☆	★★☆☆☆

WELCOME TO THE WEST RIM AND HAVASU CANYON

Separate from the national park, the western end of the canyon provides access to the canyon at two points: the West Rim, also known as Grand Canyon West, and Havasu Canyon.

1 Grand Canyon West. This destination on the West Rim is a five-hour drive from the South Rim of the Grand Canyon National Park or a 2½-hour drive from Las Vegas. Visitors arriving via Interstate 40 to Kingman, take Stockton Hill Road north to Pierce Ferry Road, and follow it to Grand Canyon West. Those traveling from Las Vegas head south on U.S. 93 to Pierce Ferry Road. In addition to the Skywalk, Grand Canyon West has a zip line, restaurant, 26 cabins, and an airport.

2 Havasu Canyon. Access into Havasu Canyon requires a permit from the Havasupai Indian Reservation, which must be secured online a year in advance. If you are lucky enough to score one, driving Historic Route 66 to Indian Route 18 is the only way to get to the Hualapai Trailhead, which descends into Havasu Canyon. There is no gas, lodging, or water at the trailhead. You can also get to the bottom by helicopter. Flights are $85 per person each way and available on a first-come, first-served basis.

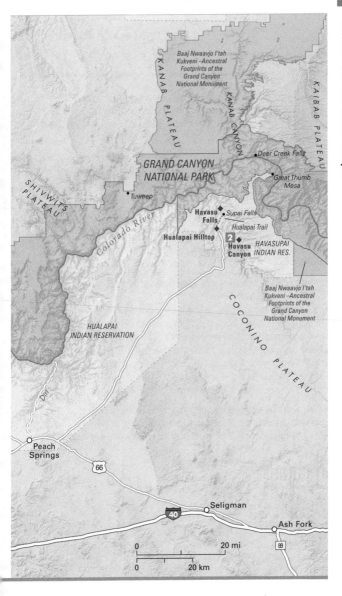

Known as the "the people of the Grand Canyon," the Pai Indians—the Havasupai and Hualapai—have lived along the Colorado River and the vast Colorado Plateau for more than 1,000 years.

These tribes seasonally moved between the plateau and the canyon, alternately hunting game and planting crops, until the establishment of reservations in the late 19th century restricted their movement.

Of the two tribes, the plateau-dwelling Hualapai (the people of the tall pines) acquired a larger chunk of traditional Pai lands with the creation of their reservation in 1883. Although the tribe has about 2,300 members, the Hualapai Reservation encompasses 108 miles of the Colorado River and a million acres of the Grand Canyon and its surrounding southern plateaus. Hualapai tribal lands include diverse habitats ranging from rolling grasslands to rugged canyons, and travel from elevations of 1,500 feet at the Colorado River to more than 7,300 feet at Aubrey Cliffs.

In recent years, the Hualapai have been attempting to foster tourism on the West Rim at Grand Canyon West—most notably with the spectacular Skywalk, a glass walkway suspended over the edge of the canyon rim. Not hampered by the regulations in place at Grand Canyon National Park, Grand Canyon West is able to offer helicopter flights down into the canyon, horseback rides to rim viewpoints, and boat trips on the Colorado River. Grand Canyon West is also the only place outside of the national park with accommodations at the rim.

While visiting native lands, be respectful of tribal laws and etiquette. Do not bring alcohol, drugs, weapons, or drones, and do not photograph tribe members without first asking permission.

Planning

When to Go

Mid-November through mid-April, when temperatures average 50 to 60 degrees Fahrenheit, is the ideal time to visit Grand Canyon West. The rest of the year, the weather hovers in the 90-degree range with a long stretch of triple-digit heat in July and August. There are few trees to provide shade or shelter from the wind, increasing exposure to the elements throughout the year. Havasu Canyon is open only February through November. Although the waterfalls and their pools will be colder in the earlier months, temperatures hiking into the canyon will be much more moderate. During the summer, from June until August, the trail is subject to closing due to flooding and extreme heat of more than 115°F. Because permits to Havasu Falls sell out within hours, visitors to the area remain roughly constant; thankfully, the tribe severely restrict the number of permits it sells to protect the canyon's fragile environment.

Getting Here and Around

AIR
Harry Reid International Airport in Las Vegas is the closest major airport to the West Rim; it is 125 miles from Grand Canyon West and 220 miles from Hualapai Hilltop, where the trail into Havasu Canyon begins. Although Kingman and the slightly closer Lake Havasu City both have airports, neither has commercial flights. Flagstaff Airport is another option. It offers multiple flights daily to and from Phoenix and Dallas-Fort Worth on American Airlines. From Flagstaff, it is 215 miles to Grand Canyon West. Scenic Airlines and Maverick Airlines fly daily from Las Vegas to the small airport at Grand Canyon West nonstop.

CAR
While you don't necessarily need a car to get from Las Vegas to Grand Canyon West, having one makes it easier to explore the region, add a visit to the South Rim, or drive a section of Route 66. If you intend to visit Havasu Canyon, a car is a must. Harry Reid International Airport's rental car center has 10 rental companies and is open 24 hours a day, 365 days a year, with continuous shuttle service to the airport terminals. Visitors to Phoenix can rent a car at Phoenix Sky Harbor International Airport Rental Car Center. Car rentals are also available on a significantly more limited basis at Flagstaff Airport. There is limited fuel service here, so fill up before leaving Interstate 40 or U.S. Highway 93, depending on the route you take.

SHUTTLE
Several companies offer shuttle tours from Las Vegas to Grand Canyon West, but there is no shuttle or bus service that isn't part of a package or tour. At Grand Canyon West, visitors are required to park and board a free hop-on, hop-off shuttle to Eagle Point,

where the Skywalk is located, and Guano Point; you can't drive a car here.

Hotels

There are limited accommodations at the West Rim since these are remote tribal lands. Grand Canyon West has 44 cabins on-site and allows RVs to spend up to three nights in its parking lot. Nearby, Grand Canyon Western Ranch offers cabins and glamping. Travelers to Havasu Canyon have limited options, too. Hualapai Lodge in Peach Springs has the only accommodations in the area for hikers and white-water rafters before or after their adventures below the rim begin. In Havasu Canyon, hikers have two options: Havasupai Lodge and the canyon's campground, both of which require reservations. Kingman, 80 miles from Grand Canyon West and 115 miles from Peach Springs, has chain hotels and Route 66–themed motels but can't compete with Las Vegas when it comes to luxury accommodations or sheer number of properties.

Restaurants

The dining scene at the West Rim is just as sparse as its accommodations. Grand Canyon West has four restaurants, including Sky View Restaurant, a meal from which can be purchased as an add-on with admission. On the way to Peach Springs or Hualapai Hilltop, there are a few decent Route 66-themed diners, but your options dwindle to Diamond Creek Restaurant at Hualapai Lodge in Peach Springs and Supai Cafe in Havasu Canyon once you enter tribal lands. Fast food chains, breweries, and mom-and-pop diners dominate the culinary scene in Kingman, but foodies will likely have to make the trek to Las Vegas to satisfy their cravings.

⇨ Hotel prices in the reviews are the lowest cost of a standard double room in high season. Restaurant prices in the reviews are the average cost of a main course at dinner, or if dinner is not served, at lunch.

What It Costs in U.S. Dollars			
$	$$	$$$	$$$$
HOTELS			
under $120	$120–$175	$176–$250	over $250
RESTAURANTS			
under $12	$12–$20	$21–$30	over $30

Tours

A number of companies provide bus tours from Las Vegas to
Grand Canyon West; at the West Rim, these guides escort you
to Eagle Point, Guano Point, and the Skywalk, sharing insights.
At one point, the Havasupai allowed tour operators into Havasu
Canyon to help carry supplies, set up camp, and act as a guide to
waterfalls, but that's no longer the case since permits are typically
snatched up by the public for the next season within hours of
becoming available on February 1.

The West Rim

 Sights

SCENIC STOPS
Eagle Point
VIEWPOINT | The heart of Grand Canyon West, this scenic overlook
is where you'll find the Skywalk, the Sky View Restaurant, a café,
replicas of Native American structures, and a shop where you can
purchase authentic Native American crafts. Hualapai musicians
and dancers perform Friday, Saturday, and Sunday from 10 am to 3
pm at the outdoor amphitheater here. ⊕ *www.grandcanyonwest.
com.*

★ Grand Canyon Skywalk
VIEWPOINT | This cantilevered glass terrace is suspended nearly
4,000 feet above the Colorado River and extends 70 feet from
the edge of the Grand Canyon. Approximately 10 feet wide, the
bridge's deck, made of tempered glass several inches thick,
has 5-foot glass railings on each side creating an unobstructed
open-air platform. Admission to the skywalk is an add-on to the
basic Grand Canyon West admission. Visitors must store personal
items, including cameras, cell phones, and video cameras, in
lockers before entering. A professional photographer takes pho-
tographs of visitors, which can be purchased from the gift shop.
⊕ *www.grandcanyonwest.com* 🖃 *$26–$30.*

Guano Point
VIEWPOINT | Named for the nitrogen-rich bat droppings (guano)
that were mined from a cave across the canyon, Guano Point
boasts the most spectacular landscapes at the West Rim. You'll
have to make a short hike from the shuttle drop-off to get to the
no-longer-functioning aerial tramway at the point, but once there,

A trip to Guano Point rewards you with panoramic views of the canyon and the river, with the Guano Point Cafe nearby for a BBQ lunch.

you'll be rewarded with nearly 360-degree views of the canyon and the river below. Guano Point Cafe serves BBQ and curried vegetables. ⊠ *Grand Canyon West*.

Hualapai Point
OTHER ATTRACTION | Formerly Hualapai Ranch, this shuttle stop now celebrates the culture of the Hualapai people. Artisans demonstrate their skills Sunday through Tuesday at Walapai Trading Post, and the Hualapai Bird Singers share their songs on the weekends. Gwe Ma'jo, the restaurant here, serves traditional dishes like pinion stew and fry bread. Hualapai Point is also where you'll find zip lines and the Cabins at Grand Canyon West. ⊕ *grandcanyonwest.com*.

TRAILS
Highpoint Hike
TRAIL | This easy, ¼-mile hike from the shuttle drop-off to the scenic overlook at Guano Point ends at a disabled aerial tramway at the rim. The tramway, which once spanned 7,500 feet across the canyon to a cave filled with nitrogen-rich bat droppings (guano), stands as a tribute to mining efforts in the canyon. Keep tabs on young hikers, and don't venture too close to the edge—there are no railings on the groomed trail. ⊠ *Grand Canyon West, Grand Canyon*.

🍴 Restaurants

Guano Point Cafe

$$$ | **AMERICAN** | This walk-up café offers a casual dining experience at Guano Point. Chow down on barbecue pork or chicken, curried vegetables, and sides like mashed potatoes and corn on the cob as you take in the canyon's views. **Known for:** panoramic views of the canyon; outdoor dining at picnic tables; limited meal options. ⓢ *Average main: $22* ✉ *Guano Point at Grand Canyon West, Grand Canyon* ⊕ *www.grandcanyonwest.com.*

Gwe Ma'jo

$$ | **AMERICAN** | Located at Hualapai Point, Gwe Ma'jo is the only restaurant at Grand Canyon West that serves breakfast, although its offerings are limited to an egg and meat plate, breakfast burrito (with or without meat), French toast, and fry bread. At lunch, you can sample Navajo dishes like pinion stew and tacos made with fry bread. **Known for:** Navajo cooking; fry-bread tacos; breakfast options. ⓢ *Average main: $15* ✉ *Hualapai Point at Grand Canyon West* ⊕ *grandcanyonwest.com.*

Sky View Restaurant

$$$ | **AMERICAN** | The only indoor, sit-down dining at Grand Canyon West overlooks the Skywalk and Eagle Point and serves chicken tenders, salads, bowls, and vegetarian burgers. Beer and wine are also available. **Known for:** floor-to-ceiling views of the Skywalk and Eagle Point; sit-down dining; meal ticket option. ⓢ *Average main: $22* ⊕ *www.grandcanyonwest.com.*

Skywalk Cafe

$$ | **AMERICAN** | This café at Eagle Point serves hamburgers, chicken sandwiches, chicken tenders, and chili dogs. Dining is outdoors with views of the Skywalk and Eagle Point or within view of the Hualapai musicians and dancers who perform several shows daily. **Known for:** American comfort food; outdoor dining; Hualapai performers. ⓢ *Average main: $16* ✉ *Eagle Point at Grand Canyon West* ⊕ *www.grandcanyonwest.com.*

Hotels

The Cabins at Grand Canyon West

$$$ | **MOTEL** | **FAMILY** | The only lodging on the West Rim, the comfortable cabins at Hualapai Ranch are clean and neat, but also small and unassuming. **Pros:** front porches with nice desert views; rustlers tell tall tales while you roast s'mores at the campfire; dining room and "saloon" serve until 4:30 pm. **Cons:** no phones or TVs; no Internet; remote setting. ⓢ *Rooms from: $236*

✉ *Quartermaster Point Rd., Grand Canyon West* ☎ *928/769–2636,
888/868–9378* ⊕ *www.grandcanyonwest.com* ⛵ *44 cabins* ⦿ *No
Meals.*

★ Grand Canyon Western Ranch

$$$$ | HOTEL | Located just 14 miles southwest of Grand Canyon
West, this historic 106,000-acre working cattle ranch sprawls
at the base of Spirit Mountain. **Pros:** variety of activities including horseback and helicopter rides; s'mores and songs around
the evening campfire; Old West experience. **Cons:** only nearby
attraction is Grand Canyon West; on-site restaurant is only option
after Grand Canyon West closes; shared bathroom facilities for
glampers. ⑤ *Rooms from: $275* ✉ *3750 E. Diamond Bar Ranch
Rd., Meadview* ☎ *928/788–0283, 800/798–0569* ⊕ *grandcanyon-
westernranch.com* ⛵ *16 lodgings* ⦿ *No Meals.*

Shopping

Creations by Native Hands Gift Shop

CRAFTS | This gift shop, at Eagle Point near the Skywalk, sells
Native American arts and crafts including jewelry. ✉ *Eagle Point at
Grand Canyon West* ⊕ *www.grandcanyonwest.com.*

Native American Flea Market

SOUVENIRS | Hualapai and other Native American artists sell their
crafts and handmade goods at Guano Point. Whether the market
is open depends on the availability of the craftsmen; you can
check on availability by calling the visitor center at ☎ *888/868–
9378.* ✉ *Guano Point at Grand Canyon West* ⊕ *grandcanyonwest.
com.*

Skywalk Main Terminal Gift Shop

SOUVENIRS | The gift shop in the Skywalk Main Terminal sells Grand
Canyon West and Route 66 T-shirts, coffee mugs, and other souvenirs. ✉ *Inside the Sywalk Main Terminal at Grand Canyon West*
⊕ *www.grandcanyonwest.com.*

Walapai Trading Post

SOUVENIRS | In addition to selling souvenirs, this shop invites
Native American artists to demonstrate their craft Sunday through
Tuesday. ⊕ *grandcanyonwest.com.*

Activities

BOATING AND RAFTING

Hualapai River Runners

WHITE-WATER RAFTING | One- and two-day river trips are offered
by the Hualapai Tribe through the Hualapai River Runners from

mid-March through October. The trips leave from Peach Springs (a two-hour drive from the West Rim) and include rafting, hiking, and transport. Meals, snacks, and beverages are provided. Children must be at least eight to take the one-day trip and 12 for the overnight trips; the rapids here are rated as Class III–VII, depending on the river flow. ⊠ *893 Hwy. 66, Peach Springs* 🕿 *928/769–2636, 888/868–9378* ⊕ *www.grandcanyonwest.com* 🕿 *From $359.*

CAMPING

There's no camping on the West Rim, but you can pitch a tent at Diamond Creek near the Colorado River.

Diamond Creek. You can camp on the banks of the Colorado River, although this beach is a noisy launch point for river runners. You'll also need a four-wheel-drive vehicle to get here. The Hualapai permit camping on their tribal lands here, with an overnight camping permit of $20 per person per night, plus taxes and fees, which can be purchased at the Hualapai Lodge. 🕿 *928/769–2227* ⊕ *hualapai-nsn.gov.*

FOUR-WHEELER TOURS

Grand Canyon Custom Tours

FOUR-WHEELING | This tour company based out of Williams offers a full-day off-road adventure to the bottom of Grand Canyon West year-round in comfortable cruisers (small luxury vans with heating and air-conditioning) rather than Jeeps. Tours leave from the Grand Canyon Railway Hotel in Williams. ⊠ *106 9th St., Williams* 🕿 *928/779–3163* ⊕ *tourstothebottom.com.*

HIKING

There are only two hikes at Grand Canyon West, neither significant. The "hike" at Eagle Point is more of a walk looping past traditionally built Native American structures. Signage along the trail describes which tribe would use the structure, how it was used, and interesting facts about it. The Highpoint Hike is an easy, ¼-mile hike from the shuttle drop-off to Guano Point jutting into the canyon. A disabled aerial tramway that once transported nitrogen-rich bat droppings (guano) from a cave 7,500 feet across the Colorado River sits on the rim there.

HORSEBACK RIDING

Unlike on the North and South rims where mules take you into the Grand Canyon, on the West Rim, horseback rides give you a taste of the Old West on trails through the desert. Wear long pants, closed-toed shoes, a hat, and sunglasses, and be sure to apply plenty of sunscreen before your ride, even in winter.

Grand Canyon Western Ranch

HORSEBACK RIDING | **FAMILY** | This ranch just 14 miles south of Grand Canyon West offers 45-minute to one-hour guided rides on quarter horses past Joshua trees and buffalo as you make your way to Sunset Hill. Riders 21 and up enjoy a Champagne toast before returning (soft drinks are available for everyone else). Although you must be at least eight years old to ride, there is no minimum height and no weight limit. Pony rides for kids seven and under as well as wagon rides pulled by Belgian draft horses are also available. ⊠ *Grand Canyon Western Ranch, 3750 E. Diamond Bar Rd., Meadview* ☎ *800/798–0569, 928/788–0283* ⊕ *grandcanyon-westernranch.com.*

SCENIC FLIGHTS

Helicopter flights depart from Las Vegas, Grand Canyon West Airport, and Grand Canyon Western Ranch. Some land at the canyon's bottom, where passengers can enjoy a picnic before reboarding; others simply fly through the canyon, pointing out sights along the way. Make reservations well in advance, as these popular tours often sell out.

Grand Canyon Scenic Airlines

AIR EXCURSIONS | In addition to flying passengers from Las Vegas to the West Rim to spend the day, Grand Canyon Scenic Airlines offers a narrated airplane tour over the canyon with hotel pickup and drop-off. ⊠ *Las Vegas* ☎ *702/638–3300* ⊕ *www.scenic.com.*

Grand Canyon Western Ranch

AIR EXCURSIONS | **FAMILY** | Originating from a ranch 14 miles south of Grand Canyon West, this tour flies through the canyon at an altitude approximately 2,000 feet below the rim. As you soar in the air, watch for rafters on the river and wildlife, including elk and wild horses. ⊠ *Grand Canyon Western Ranch, 3750 E. Diamond Bar Rd., Meadview* ☎ *928/788–0283* ⊕ *www.grandcanyonwest-ernranch.com.*

Maverick Helicopters

AIR EXCURSIONS | **FAMILY** | Descend 3,500 feet below the rim on this ECO-Star helicopter tour that takes off from Grand Canyon West Airport. After landing 300 feet above the Colorado, you'll have 20 minutes to take photographs and marvel at the canyon before heading back to the rim. ⊠ *Grand Canyon West Airport* ☎ *702/728–4241* ⊕ *www.maverickairlines.com.*

Papillon

AIR EXCURSIONS | These narrated helicopter flights to the West Rim—with a landing at the bottom or without—take off from Papillon's terminal at Harry Reid International Airport with complimentary pickup and drop-off from major Las Vegas hotels available. Several upgrades are available, including a VIP Sky-walk experience. ⊠ *Boulder City Municipal Airport, Boulder City* ☎ *702/736–7243* ⊕ *www.papillon.com.*

ZIP-LINING

The Zip Line at Grand Canyon West

ZIP-LINING | Available from Hualapai Ranch, the Zip Line at Grand Canyon West has two runs, each with four lines. The first run gets your heart pumping with a 1,000-plus-foot sail across a portion of the canyon; the second is faster and longer, roughly 2,000 feet. Riders must weigh at least 90 pounds but less than 275 pounds, and children under the age of 18 must be accompanied by a legal guardian. Grand Canyon West may suspend operation of the zip line if there are high winds, thunder, lightning, or rain. ⊠ *Grand Canyon West* ☎ *928/769–2636* ⊕ *www.grandcanyonwest.com* 🎫 *$44.*

Havasu Canyon

141 miles northwest from Williams to the head of Hualapai Hilltop.

With the establishment of Grand Canyon National Park in 1919, the Havasupai ("people of the blue-green water") were confined to their summer village of Supai and the surrounding 518 acres in the 5-mile-wide and 12-mile-long Havasu Canyon. In 1975 the reservation was substantially enlarged but is still completely surrounded by national park lands on all but its southern border. Each year about 25,000 tourists fly, hike, or ride into Havasu Canyon to visit the Havasupai. Despite their economic reliance on tourism, the Havasupai take their guardianship of the Grand Canyon seriously and severely limit visitation in order to protect the fragile canyon habitats. Dubbed the "Shangri-la of the Grand Canyon," the waterfalls have drawn visitors to this remote reservation.

Major flooding in 2008 altered Havasu Canyon's famous landscape, and it was closed to visitors for almost 10 months. Supai reopened in 2009, but water and mud damage have changed some of the beautiful waterfalls, their streams and pools, and the amount of blue-green travertine.

■ TIP→ **Visiting Havasu Canyon requires preparation: Reservations and permits must be obtained well in advance. Camping reservations, which usually sell out in a few hours, can be made online only beginning February 1 for the following year (⊕ *havasupaireservations.com*); Havasupai Lodge reservations can be made by phone only beginning June 1 for the following year (☎ *928/448–2111*).**

Did You Know?

Havasu Canyon has five waterfalls but the most famous—and most photographed—is Havasu Falls, known for its large turquoise pools. But if you want to see it you'll have to plan well in advance—reservations are required to venture into the canyon.

GETTING HERE AND AROUND

Hualapai Hilltop is reached via Indian Route 18, which you follow about 65 miles north from historic Route 66 (34 miles west of Seligman and 50 miles east of Kingman). The total driving distance from the South Rim of the Grand Canyon is about 200 miles and takes about four hours; it's roughly 170 miles from Flagstaff to Hualapai Hilltop. The closest lodging and services are in Peach Springs, a 90-minute drive, and Seligman, about 2 hours away.

The Havasupai restrict the number of visitors to the canyon; you must obtain entrance permits and make reservations well in advance.

■ TIP→ **You will be stopped and turned away if you don't have a reservation!**

The Hualapai Trail begins at Hualapai Hilltop. You can park your car here (the parking lot is patrolled), but there is no gas, lodging, or water available at the trailhead. From an elevation of 5,200 feet, the 8-mile trail travels down a moderate grade to Supai Village at 3,200 feet. Bring plenty of water and food, and avoid hiking during the middle of the day, when canyon temperatures can reach into the 100s. No day hiking is permitted; campers must pay for three nights. If you prefer to have a bed and plumbing, the Havasupai Lodge is in the village, along with a small grocery store and a café. The campground is 2 miles farther, closer to the waterfalls. Permits and camping reservations for the year ahead may be purchased online only beginning February 1 (⊕ *havasupaireservations.com*); Havasupai Lodge reservations can be made by phone beginning June 1 (☎ *928/448–2111*).

Another option is a helicopter ride into the canyon with Air West Helicopters. Flights leave from Hualapai Hilltop four days a week during summer and two days a week during winter, and cost $85 per person each way. Reservations aren't accepted, and visitors are transported on a first-come, first-served basis. Tribal members and supplies are boarded prior to tourists, so you are not guaranteed a ride down (or back up).

WHEN TO GO

Havasu Canyon is open only to visitors with permits for the tourist season, February through November. Spring is usually the best time to go since canyon temperatures haven't topped triple digits yet, and the waters at the base of the falls aren't as frigid as they can be earlier in the season. Runoff from snow melt also increases the water flow over the falls. In the early summer, you'll want to get an early start on the Hualapai Trail to avoid the midday heat as much as possible. July to September is monsoon season, when heavy rains can cause flash flooding that forces the canyon's closure. Because visiting Havasu Canyon is by permit only and those permits sell out, crowds are roughly the same no matter when you go.

ESSENTIALS

TRANSPORTATION CONTACTS Airwest Helicopters. ☎ *623/516– 2790* ⊕ *www.airwesthelicopters.com.*

VISITOR INFORMATION Havasupai Tourist Enterprise. ☎ *928/448– 2121* ⊕ *theofficialhavasupaitribe.com.*

 Sights

SCENIC DRIVES
Route 66

SCENIC DRIVE | Navigating the longest continuous stretch of drivable Route 66 is the only way to get to Havasu Canyon. While not a particularly scenic drive, diners serving burgers and shakes, roadside attractions like Grand Canyon Caverns, and Burma Shave signs with catchy sayings make it a worthwhile, nostalgic trip. From Interstate 40, take Exit 123 at Seligman or Exit 53 in Kingman. The 87-mile drive connects the two communities, with Peach Springs and Indian Route 18, the road to Hualapai Hilltop and Havasu Canyon roughly at the midway point. Before you exit the interstate, fill up your tank; there are few gas stations between Seligman and Kingman.

SCENIC STOPS
Havasu Canyon

CANYON | South of the middle part of the Grand Canyon National Park's South Rim and away from the crowds, Havasu Canyon is the home of the Havasupai, a tribe that has lived in this isolated area for centuries. You'll discover why they are known as the "people of the blue-green waters" when you see the canyon's waterfalls— **Fifty Foot Falls**, **Little Navajo Falls**, **Havasu Falls**, **Beaver Falls**, and **Mooney Falls**. Accumulated travertine formations in some of the most popular pools were washed out in massive flooding decades ago and again in 2008 and 2010, but it's still a magical place.

The village of Supai, which currently has about 200 tribal residents, is accessed by the 8-mile-long Hualapai Trail, which drops 2,000 feet from the canyon rim to the tiny town.

To reach Havasu's waterfalls, you must hike downstream from the village of Supai. Pack adequate food and supplies. There is a café and a trading post in the village, but prices for food and sundries are more than double what they would be outside the reservation.

The tribe does not allow alcohol, drugs, pets, drones, or weapons. Reservations are necessary for camping or staying at Havasupai Lodge. ⊠ *Havasupai Tribe Tourism, Supai* ☎ *928/448–2121 general info, 928/448–2201 lodging reservations* ⊕ *www.facebook.com/HavasupaiTribeTourismOfficial.*

Mail by Mule

Arguably the most remote mail route in the United States follows a steep 8-mile trail to the tiny town of Supai in Havasu Canyon. Havasupai tribal members living deep within the confines of the Grand Canyon rely on this route for the delivery of everything from food to furniture. During a typical week, more than a ton of mail is sent into the canyon by mule, with each animal carrying a cargo of about 130 pounds.

★ Havasu Falls

WATERFALL | Havasu Canyon has five major waterfalls. The first three—Fifty Foot Falls, Little Navajo Falls, and Havasu Falls—sit between the village of Supai and the Havasu Falls Campground; Mooney Falls and Beaver Falls are past the campground on the way to the confluence of the Colorado River. Often overlooked because it's a short trek off Hualapai Trail, **Fifty Foot Falls** typically has fewer crowds than **Little Navajo Falls**, roughly 30 feet farther down Havasu Creek. The large turquoise pools of **Havasu Falls** make a great place to cool off with a swim. Getting to the waterfalls past the campground becomes a little more challenging. Water spray from **Mooney Falls,** a ½ mile from the campground, makes the descent to its base slick, especially on the rock stairs near the end. But the effort rewards with awe-inspiring views of the water plunging 190 feet into a colorful pool. **Beaver Falls** is another 2 miles farther down the trail and offers multiple swimming holes. Visitors often bring inflatable water tubes to float in the pools, in addition to extra towels and plenty of sunscreen. Water shoes for walking on slippery travertine are highly recommended. ⊠ *Havasupai Tribe Tourism, Supai* ☎ *928/448–2121* ⊕ *theofficialhavasupaitribe.com.*

TRAILS

★ Hualapai Trail

TRAIL | The trail in and out of Havasu Canyon begins at Hualapai Hilltop, 90 minutes from Peach Springs, and drops about 1,800 feet in the first 2 miles, followed by 1½ miles of switchbacks. The remaining 4½ miles to the tiny village of Supai (a total of 8 miles from the trailhead parking lot) is relatively flat. From Supai, the trail begins to parallel Havasu Creek and passes the first three major waterfalls: Fifty Foot Falls, Little Navajo Falls, and Havasu Falls.

The Hualapai Trails can be hiked or visited via mule train—either way be prepared for jaw-dropping scenery.

Havasu Falls Campground sits 10 miles from the trailhead (2 miles from Supai), but the trail continues. Just a ½ mile from the campground is Mooney Falls, which requires navigating rocks slick with water spray to get to its base. Two miles past that, Beaver Falls is the last major waterfall on the trail, but hikers can continue all the way to the confluence of the Colorado River on the Hualapai Trail, an additional 4 miles. In total, the Hualapai Trail is 12 miles each way from Hualapai Hilltop to Beaver Falls (16 miles to the Colorado River). You must have a permit to enter Havasu Canyon or you will be turned away. Hualapai Trail is not a day hike; you must have reservations either at Havasupai Lodge or the campground before you go. Because there is no available drinking water on the trail, you will have to bring your own. Packing mules can be arranged in advance to carry your gear in and out of the canyon (give them the right of way on the trail) through the Havasupai Tribe Tourism, and helicopter rides are available for $85 on a first-come, first-served basis for visitors who don't feel they can hike back out. ✉ *Havasupai Tribe Tourism, Supai* ☎ *928/448–2121* 🌐 *theofficialhavasupaitribe.com* ⏲ *Closed Dec. and Jan.*

Hotels

Havasupai Lodge

$$$$ | **HOTEL** | Operated by the Havasupai Tribe at the bottom of Havasu Canyon, these are fairly spartan accommodations—each room has two double beds and a bathroom—but you won't mind

much when you see the natural beauty surrounding you. **Pros:** sleep in a bed rather than a tent; Native American perspective on the natural and cultural history of the Grand Canyon; private bathroom. **Cons:** more than a 2-mile hike to the falls; plain and worn rooms; no phones, Internet, or TVs. ⑤ *Rooms from: $660* ✉ *159 Supai, Supai* ☎ *928/448–2111, 928/448–2201* ⊕ *theofficialhavasu-paitribe.com* ⇴ *24 rooms* ⦿ *No Meals.*

Hualapai Lodge

$$$ | HOTEL | In Peach Springs on the longest stretch of the original historic Route 66, the hotel has clean, basic rooms and a comfortable lobby with a large fireplace that is welcoming on chilly nights. **Pros:** concierge desk arranges river trips with the Hualapai River Runners; good on-site restaurant, Diamond Creek, with Native American dishes; Hualapai locals add a different perspective to the canyon experience. **Cons:** basic rooms lack historic charm; location off the beaten path; train passes every 15 minutes and blows its horn. ⑤ *Rooms from: $185* ✉ *900 Rte. 66, Peach Springs* ☎ *928/769–2230, 888/868–9378* ⊕ *www.grandcanyon-west.com* ⇴ *54 rooms* ⦿ *No Meals.*

 Activities

CAMPING

Havasu Canyon. You can stay in the primitive campgrounds in Havasu Canyon for $395 per person per night (a three-night stay is required and permits are included). Reservations are difficult to get; they go on sale February 1 for the following year and sell out within a few hours. ☎ *928/448–2121, 928/448–2180* ⊕ *havasu-paireservations.com.*

HIKING

Besides swimming in the waterfalls' pools, hiking is the only real activity in the canyon. You'll need a permit, obtained ahead of time through ⊕ *havasupaireservations.com.* Keep that permit with you as you hike the Hualapai Trail as there are several checkpoints along the way to make sure everyone has paid. There is no water on the trail, so pack enough to stay hydrated on your way to Supai, where you can purchase more, or to the campground, where more is available. Ideally, bring enough water with you to last your entire stay. All hiking, especially between Supai and Hualapai Hilltop, should be completed early in the day since temperatures often top 100 degrees Fahrenheit in the canyon.

Chapter 6

6

GATEWAYS

Updated by
Teresa Bitler

🏕 Camping   🏨 Hotels   🏃 Activities   👁 Scenery   👥 Crowds
★★★☆☆   ★★★☆☆   ★★★★★   ★★★★☆   ★★★★☆

WELCOME TO GATEWAYS

TOP REASONS TO GO

★ **Hotels and restaurants:** Accommodations are hard to come by in the national park and dining options are limited. These communities have plenty of both.

★ **Route 66:** Get your kicks on the Mother Road in downtown Flagstaff and Williams or on your way to the West Rim.

★ **The great outdoors:** Nature lovers can hike, bike, fish, horseback ride, camp, stargaze, ski, and explore the Cococino National Forest by ATV.

★ **Native American crafts:** Authentic jewelry, pottery, baskets, and other crafts line the shelves of the Cameron Trading Post, museum gift shops, and local outlets.

★ **Animal encounters:** See black bears at Bearizona, deer at the Grand Canyon Deer Farm, and raptors and other birds at Raptor Ranch.

1 **Tusayan.** A tiny community close to the South Rim entrance.

2 **Valle (Grand Canyon Junction).** A hot spot for unique accommodations, including luxury trailer rentals.

3 **Williams.** The "Gateway to the Grand Canyon" offers Route 66 nostalgia and a train to the South Rim.

4 **Flagstaff.** The largest city in northern Arizona has a lively historic district, trendy restaurants, and access to outdoor adventures.

5 **Cameron.** Known for its historic trading post, scenic gorge, and Native American culture.

6 **Lees Ferry.** This section of the Colorado River is the launch for most Grand Canyon rafting trips, and also draws fishing enthusiasts hoping to hook a world-class trout.

7 **Jacob Lake.** A small town high in pine country.

8 **Fredonia.** On the Utah border, this small town founded by Mormons in 1885 bills itself as the "Gateway to the North Rim."

9 **Marble Canyon.** Stretch your legs on the original Navajo Bridge over Marble Canyon, or hit the trails at Vermillion Cliffs National Monument.

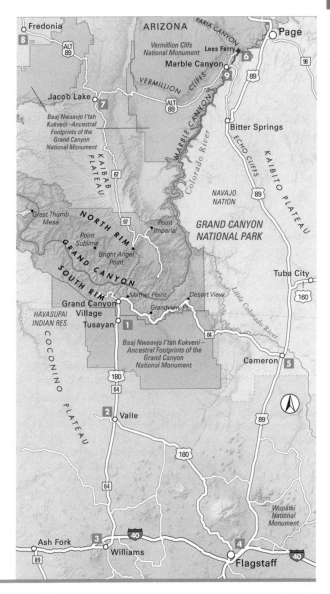

Fredonia

ARIZONA

PARIA CANYON

Page

8

ALT 89

Vermillion Cliffs
National Monument

Lees Ferry

6

Marble Canyon

9

98

VERMILLION CLIFFS

Jacob Lake

7

ALT 89

Baaj Nwaavjo I'tah
Kukveni –Ancestral
Footprints of the
Grand Canyon
National Monument

MARBLE CANYON

Bitter Springs

ECHO CLIFFS

KAIBITO PLATEAU

89

KAIBAB PLATEAU

67

Colorado River

NAVAJO
NATION

GRAND CANYON
NATIONAL PARK

Great Thumb
Mesa

NORTH RIM

67

Point
Imperial

GRAND CANYON

Point
Sublime

Bright Angel
Point

SOUTH RIM

Mather Point

Tuba City

Desert View

Little Colorado River

160

Grand Canyon
Village

Grandview Pt.

HAVASUPAI
INDIAN RES.

Tusayan

1

Baaj Nwaavjo I'tah Kukveni –
Ancestral Footprints of the
Grand Canyon
National Monument

64

Cameron

5

COCONINO PLATEAU

180

64

2

Valle

89

180

64

Wupatki
National
Monument

I-40

Ash Fork

3

40

89

Williams

4

Flagstaff

40

Despite its magnificence, the Grand Canyon remained a well-kept secret until the Santa Fe Railroad built a line from Williams to the South Rim in 1901. A year later, the first automobile arrived at the Grand Canyon after an arduous two-day journey from Flagstaff. In the 1950s, the current highway from Williams was built, and a few years later visitation to the park exceeded one million. Today, roughly six million people visit the Grand Canyon, and most of these head to the more accessible South Rim.

Just 1 mile south of the entrance station, the tiny community of Tusayan offers basic amenities and an airport that serves as a starting point for airplane and helicopter tours of the canyon. Less than 60 miles south on Highway 64, the cozy mountain town of Williams lives up to its reputation as the "Gateway to the Grand Canyon." Founded in 1882 when the railroad passed through, it was once a rough-and-tumble joint, replete with saloons and bordellos. Today it reflects a much milder side of the Wild West, with 3,200 residents and more than 30 hotels and motels. Wander along Main Street and indulge in Route 66 nostalgia inside antiques shops or souvenir and T-shirt stores.

At the junction of Interstate 40 (east and west) and Interstate 17 (heading south toward Phoenix), Flagstaff makes a good base for combined explorations of the South Rim and the other natural and cultural wonders on the Colorado Plateau. If you are heading to the Eastern Entrance on the South Rim or to the North Rim via U.S. 89 from Flagstaff, Cameron makes a worthwhile stop. You'll find a trading post, gas station, post office, restaurant, and a historic lodge.

Marble Canyon, to the north of Tuba City, marks the geographical beginning of the Grand Canyon at its northeastern tip. It's a good stopping point if you're driving U.S. 89 to the North Rim. En route from the South Rim to the North Rim is Lees Ferry, where most of the area's river rafts start their journey. Fredonia, a small community of about 1,100, approximately an hour's drive north of the Grand Canyon, is often referred to as the gateway to the North Rim; it's also relatively close to Zion and Bryce Canyon national parks. The tiny town of Jacob Lake, nestled high in pine country at an elevation of 7,925 feet, was named after Mormon explorer Jacob Hamblin, also known as the "Buckskin Missionary." Not much more than a lodge and RV park, Jacob Lake is mostly just an en route point for visitors heading to the final 45 miles on Highway 67 to the North Rim.

Planning

Hotels

Accommodations in the gateway communities are a mixed bag. In Tusayan, minutes from the South Rim's entrance, chain hotels line Highway 64, while in Valle (Grand Canyon Junction) you'll find upscale glamping at Under Canvas and Clear Sky Resort. By far, Flagstaff has the most lodging options, from massive name-brand hotels near the campus of Northern Arizona University to historic hotels downtown and bed-and-breakfasts. As you drive from Flagstaff to the North Rim, motels with a restaurant, small store, and gas station (if you're lucky) are your only option. Fredonia has some vacation rentals, including cabins, but if you want to stay in an area hotel, you're better off booking a room across the state line in Kanab, Utah, just 7 miles away, where you can stay at chains, boutique hotels, and bed-and-breakfasts.

Restaurants

You'll find lots of comfort foods in the communities south of the canyon: barbecue restaurants, steak houses, and burger joints predominate. If you're looking for something different, Flagstaff has good multiethnic and vegan options, upscale restaurants with extensive wine lists, and a thriving craft brewery scene. Since the land east of the national park is part of the Navajo Nation, restaurants in Cameron and Marble Canyon serve Native American favorites like fry bread, chili, and beef stew as well as burgers and sandwiches. Closer to the North Rim, the menus again slant toward comfort foods, and the restaurants tend to be no-frills mom-and-pop places. Some restaurants in these gateway communities north, south, and east of the canyon close in the winter, especially during January and February, so call ahead.

⇨ *Hotel prices in the reviews are the lowest cost of a standard double room in high season. Restaurant prices in the reviews are the average cost of a main course at dinner, or if dinner is not served, at lunch.*

What It Costs in U.S. Dollars			
$	$$	$$$	$$$$
HOTELS			
under $120	$120–$175	$176–$250	over $250
RESTAURANTS			
under $12	$12–$20	$21–$30	over $30

Tusayan

57 miles north of Williams, 2 miles south of Grand Canyon National Park.

The small hamlet of Tusayan, incorporated as a town only in 2010, is little more than a place to sleep and eat when visiting the Grand Canyon's South Rim. The main attractions here are an IMAX theater and visitor center, where you can see a film about the canyon and purchase tickets for air and jeep tours, and the Grand Canyon Airport, the takeoff point for plane and helicopter tours.

GETTING HERE AND AROUND

Tusayan's quarter-mile strip of hotels, eateries, and services sits right on Highway 64, the road leading into Grand Canyon National Park. Parking lots are plentiful.

Sights

Grand Canyon Visitor Center

VISITOR CENTER | FAMILY | Here you can get information about activities and tours and buy a national park pass, which enables you to skip past some of the crowds and access the park by special entry lanes. Nevertheless, the biggest draw is the six-story IMAX screen that features the short movie *Grand Canyon: Rivers of Time.* You can learn about the geologic and natural history of the canyon, soar above stunning rock formations, and ride the rapids through the rocky gorge. The film is shown every hour on the half hour; the adjoining gift store is huge and well stocked. ⊠ *450 Hwy. 64/U.S. 180, Grand Canyon* ⊹ *2 miles south of the Grand Canyon's south entrance* ☎ *928/638–2468* ⊕ *explorethecanyon. com* 🎫 *$13.59 for IMAX movies.*

🍴 Restaurants

The Coronado Room

$$$ | AMERICAN | This restaurant inside the Best Western Grand Canyon Squire Inn delivers well-prepared, hearty American food, with an emphasis on meat (steak, chicken, and pork), plus elk chili and fry bread, sandwiches, and flan. There's a good-size wine list, too. **Known for:** Tusayan's best wine list; splurge-worthy dining; mix of upscale and casual entrées. ⑤ *Average main: $24 ⊠ 74 Hwy. 64/U.S. 180, Grand Canyon* ☎ *928/638–2681* ⊕ *www.grandcanyonsquire.com* ⊗ *No lunch.*

Plaza Bonita

$$ | MEXICAN | FAMILY | One of a chain of Mexican restaurants spread throughout the state, this location dishes up standard south-of-the-border fare like enchiladas, nachos, and shredded beef burritos, as well as more unique offerings such as snapper Veracruz and mole. Save room for dessert; the impressive menu has all the Mexican restaurant staples, from churros and flan to deep-fried ice cream. **Known for:** one of the best bars for cocktails in Tusayan; discount for paying in cash or staying at Red Feather Lodge next door; gluten-free and vegetarian dishes. ⑤ *Average main: $20 ⊠ 352 Hwy. 64/U.S. 180, Grand Canyon* ☎ *928/638–8900* ⊕ *myplazabonitatusayan.com.*

☕ Coffee and Quick Bites

Foodie Club

$$ | AMERICAN | FAMILY | An alternative to the area's fast-food chains, this gourmet sandwich shop and diner serves traditional and Latin American–inspired breakfast and lunch all day. Order a breakfast burrito, pancakes, or eggs before heading into the park, or down a hot or cold sandwich, torta, or french fries topped with carne asada when you return. **Known for:** fresh, quality food served quickly; gluten-free and vegetarian options; grab-and-go items. ⑤ *Average main: $15 ⊠ 400 Hwy. 64/U.S. 180, Grand Canyon* ☎ *928/638–3115* ⊕ *thefoodieclubs.com.*

Grand Canyon Chocolate Factory

$ | DESSERTS | FAMILY | Across the street from the Grand Canyon Visitor Center and IMAX theater, this sweet shop sells 15 different flavors of truffles, 18 types of fudge, 24 flavors of gelato, candy, popcorn, trail mix, and caramel apples. **Known for:** everything but gelato made on-site; trail mix for a Grand Canyon hike; tasty fudge flavors. ⑤ *Average main: $5 ⊠ 469 Hwy. 64, Grand Canyon* ☎ *928/853–9753.*

Hotels

Best Western Grand Canyon Squire Inn

$$$$ | **HOTEL** | **FAMILY** | About 2 miles from the park's south entrance, this motel lacks the historic charm of the lodges at the canyon rim but has more amenities, including pools, a bowling alley, a gym, a small cowboy museum, and one of the better restaurants in the region. **Pros:** cool pools in summer and a hot tub for cold winter nights; copious children's activities at the Family Fun Center; rooms have refrigerators, microwaves, and coffeemakers. **Cons:** hall noise can be an issue with all of the in-hotel activities; very large (and bustling) property; rooms near pool can be especially noisy. ⑤ *Rooms from: $269* ⊠ *74 Hwy. 64/U.S. 180, Grand Canyon* ☎ *928/638–2681, 800/622–6966* ⊕ *www.grandcanyonsquire.com* ⤳ *318 rooms* ⦿❘ *No Meals.*

The Grand Hotel

$$$$ | **HOTEL** | **FAMILY** | At the south end of Tusayan, this popular, Xanterra-managed hotel has bright, clean, and contemporary rooms, a cozy stone-and-timber lobby, and free Wi-Fi. **Pros:** managed by park and resort management company Xanterra; gift shop stocked with art, outdoor gear, and regional books; 20 Tesla and two universal charging stations. **Cons:** somewhat generic property; on-site restaurant is uninspired and overpriced; indoor pool only. ⑤ *Rooms from: $325* ⊠ *149 Hwy. 64/U.S. 180, Grand Canyon* ☎ *928/638–3333, 888/634–7263* ⊕ *www.grandcanyonlodges.com* ⤳ *121 rooms* ⦿❘ *No Meals.*

Holiday Inn Express Grand Canyon

$$$$ | **HOTEL** | A little more than a mile from the south entrance gate, this reliable hotel offers clean rooms, a free breakfast, and a heated pool and hot tub to work the knots out of sore muscles after a long hike. **Pros:** adults-only building; heated indoor pool and hot tub; clean, comfortable rooms. **Cons:** expensive for what you get; thin walls make for a noisy stay; some rooms could use an update. ⑤ *Rooms from: $299* ⊠ *226 Hwy. 64/U.S. 180, Grand Canyon* ☎ *928/683–3000* ⊕ *www.ihg.com* ⤳ *196 rooms* ⦿❘ *Free Breakfast.*

★ Red Feather Lodge

$$$ | **HOTEL** | About 6 miles from the canyon, this clean, family-run lodge has a two-story motel building and a newer, three-story hotel building, both good values. **Pros:** lower-priced than most lodging close to park; pet-friendly; pool and hot tub. **Cons:** stairs only in the two-story motel; motel rooms have showers (hotel rooms have shower/tubs); only two devices per room allowed on Wi-Fi at a time. ⑤ *Rooms from: $200* ⊠ *300 Hwy. 64/U.S. 180,*

Grand Canyon ☎ *928/638–2414, 800/538–2345* ⊕ *www.redfeath-erlodge.com* ⤴ *215 rooms* ¶⬤ *No Meals.*

 # Shopping

Grand Canyon Trading Post

SOUVENIRS | Locally made hot sauces, Grand Canyon–themed T-shirts, and stuffed desert animals are just a few of the items you'll find at this gift shop. Along the back wall, a section is devoted to Native American crafts, predominantly jewelry and pottery. ✉ *337 Hwy. 64, Grand Canyon* ☎ *928/638–2418.*

 # Activities

Apache Stables

HORSEBACK RIDING | FAMILY | There's nothing like a horseback ride to immerse you in the Western experience. From stables near Tusayan, these folks offer gentle horses and a ride through the forest. Choose from one- and two-hour trail rides (March–October) or the popular campfire rides and horse-drawn wagon excursions (late May–early September). ✉ *Forest Service Rd. 328, Grand Canyon* ✛ *1 mile north of Tusayan* ☎ *928/638–2891* ⊕ *www.apachestables.com* ⤴ *From $59.*

Grand Canyon Rentals Adventures

FOUR-WHEELING | FAMILY | Explore the Kaibab National Forest using navigation tablets loaded with popular routes through the ponderosa pine trees. Rentals of the two-, and four-seat ATVs include sanitized helmets, goggles, balaclava masks, water, ice chest, and ice packs and range from a two-hour minimum to 24 hours. ✉ *Grand Canyon National Park Airport, 3551 Airport Rd., Grand Canyon* ☎ *928/220–5907* ⊕ *www.grandcanyon-rentals.com* ⤴ *From $350 for a 2-hour rental of a 2-seat ATV.*

Tusayan Bike Trail

BIKING | Pedal the depths of the Kaibab National Forest on the Tusayan Bike Trails System (also known locally as the Greenway Trail). Following linked loop trails at an elevation of 6,750 feet, you can bike as few as 3 miles or as many as 38 miles round-trip along old logging roads (some parts are paved) through ponderosa pine forest and the national park. Keep an eye out for elk, mule deer, hawks, eagles, pronghorn antelope, turkeys, coyote, and porcupines. Open for biking year-round (but most feasible March through October), the trail is accessed on the north side of the IMAX parking lot or on the west side of Highway 64, a half-mile north of Tusayan. ✉ *Tusayan Ranger District, Grand Canyon* ☎ *928/638–2443* ⊕ *www.fs.usda.gov/recarea/kaibab.*

CAMPING

Grand Canyon Camper Village and RV Park

CAMPGROUND | More of a city than a village, this popular RV park and campground has 200 utility hookups and 50 tent sites. Reservations are a good idea during the busy spring and summer seasons. Coin-operated laundry is available on-site. ⊠ 549 Camper Village La., Grand Canyon ☎ 928/638–2887 ⊕ www.grandcanyoncampervillage.com ☜ Tent sites are $20 per night; RV from $45 per night.

Ten X Campground

CAMPGROUND | Two miles south of Tusayan, this campground offers 142 single sites with water and pit toilets, but no electrical hookups or showers, plus two group sites. Most campsites are reservable, including the two group sites, one that accommodates 100 campers and the other 50. Thirty single sites are available first-come, first-served only. Unlike campgrounds in the park itself, campfires are allowed. Learn about the surrounding ponderosa pine forest on a self-guided nature trail, or check out one of the evening ranger-led programs. ⊠ Grand Canyon ✛ 9 miles south of the park, east of Hwy. 64 ⊕ www.recreation.gov ☜ Standard sites from $20.

Valle (Grand Canyon Junction)

29 miles south of Grand Canyon National Park, 50 miles west of Flagstaff.

Located at the junction of Highway 64 and U.S. 180, this unincorporated community hasn't had much appeal until Under Canvas and Clear Sky Resorts began offering glamping and Raptor Ranch opened as a birds-of-prey attraction with an attached RV park and campground. More is anticipated in the near future. Although Valle (pronounced "Valley") petitioned for a name change to Grand Canyon Junction, the Arizona State Board on Geographic and Historic Names recently denied the request. Still, the area appears as Grand Canyon Junction on Google Maps. Ironically, to make things even more confusing, properties in Valle have a Williams address even though Williams is 30 miles away.

GETTING HERE AND AROUND

From Williams, head north on Highway 64 approximately 30 miles. Valle (Grand Canyon Junction) sits at the intersection of Highway 64 and U.S. 180. If you are coming from Flagstaff, take U.S. 180 northwest out of the downtown area 50 miles to Highway 64. To get to Grand Canyon National Park, continue 29 miles north on Highway 64 through Tusayan to the south entrance.

Sights

Raptor Ranch

CITY PARK | FAMILY | Falconers Troy Morris and Ron Brown purchased this former *Flintstones*-themed attraction in 2019 and today offer raptor encounters, flight demonstrations, and educational programs, including falconry classes. Visitors can interact with the more than 50 birds here, walk through Bedrock City, and pose with concrete Flintstone characters. The property is still being renovated—it recently added a pizza and chicken joint, Fred's Diner—but it is definitely worth the $8 to stretch your legs and let the kids blow off steam. ⊠ *332 Hwy. 64, Grand Canyon* ☎ *928/635–3072* ⊕ *raptor-ranch.com* 🖼 *$8.*

Restaurants

Grand Canyon Inn Restaurant

$$ | AMERICAN | This no-frills restaurant at the Grand Canyon Inn plates all-American fare like pork chops, fried chicken, and burgers. Pasta and salads are available, too. **Known for:** one of the few restaurants in the area; open for breakfast, lunch, and dinner; better than expected meals. 💲 *Average main: $15* ⊠ *Grand Canyon Inn, 257 S. Hwy. 64, Grand Canyon* ☎ *928/635–9203* ⊕ *www.grandcanyoninn.com.*

Coffee and Quick Bites

Fred's Diner

$$ | FAST FOOD | FAMILY | Tucked in the back of the Raptor Ranch gift shop, this order-at-the-counter eatery is the area's best option for a quick bite on the road. Pizza dominates the menu, but chicken tenders and wings are options, too. **Known for:** a quick bite on the road; pizza and chicken tenders; part of the Raptor Ranch roadside attraction. 💲 *Average main: $12* ⊠ *332 South State Hwy. 64, Grand Canyon* ☎ *928/635–3072* ⊕ *raptor-ranch.com/freds-diner-at-raptor-ranch.*

🛏 Hotels

★ Clear Sky Resort

$$$$ | RESORT | These self-contained, climate-controlled domes on the edge of Valle are the ultimate in glamping, with themes ranging from "Grand Canyon" to "80s Video Games." Guests enjoy panoramic views from their dome's enormous window as well as deck hammocks, skylight with telescope for stargazing, and a swinging chair for relaxing. **Pros:** 1,000-square-foot panoramic window; climate-controlled domes with private bathrooms; frisbee golf, happy hour, live music, and more. **Cons:** views are of the high desert, not the Grand Canyon; priciest accommodations in the area; no pets allowed. ⑤ *Rooms from: $400* ✉ *629 Highgrove Rd., Grand Canyon* ☎ *888/704–4445* ⊕ *grandcanyon.clearskyresorts.com* 🛏 *40 domes* ⑩ *No Meals.*

★ Under Canvas Grand Canyon

$$$ | **RESORT** | Guests stay in safari-style tents while enjoying five-star amenities like luxury linens, hot showers, gourmet food, and organic bath products. **Pros:** glamping with luxury touches; very good on-site dining; evening campfire with s'mores. **Cons:** extremely washboarded road leading into the camp; no Wi-Fi or electricity; only some tents have private bathrooms. ⑤ *Rooms from: $250* ✉ *979 Airpark La., Grand Canyon* ☎ *928/504–4404, 877/462–0648* ⊕ *www.undercanvas.com/camps/grand-canyon* 🛏 *91 tents* ⑩ *No Meals.*

Shopping

Rocks & More

SOUVENIRS | The emphasis is on more at this rock shop in Valle. Not only does it stock precious stones, geodes, and fossils, it sells Native American jewelry, metalwork, landscape decor, and cool souvenirs. ✉ *317 Hwy. 64, Grand Canyon* ☎ *928/635–1522.*

Activities

Raptor Ranch Campground

CAMPGROUND | **FAMILY** | This next-door neighbor to the Raptor Ranch birds-of-prey attraction has 37 RV spaces and three tent-only sites. Campers are invited to watch free raptor flight demonstrations, and the young-at-heart can climb on *Flintstones*-themed playground equipment at Bedrock City. There's also an on-site store, restaurant, showers, and dump station. ✉ *332 Hwy. 64, Grand Canyon* ☎ *928/635–3072* ⊕ *raptor-ranch.com.*

Flagstaff

146 miles northwest of Phoenix, 27 miles north of Sedona via Oak Creek Canyon.

Few travelers slow down long enough to explore Flagstaff, a city of 77,000 known locally as "Flag"; most stop only to spend the night at one of the town's many motels before making the last leg of the trip to the Grand Canyon, 80 miles north. Flag makes

The Arizona Snowbowl isn't just for winter; the chairlift has great views year-round.

a good base for day trips to ancient Native American sites and the Navajo and Hopi reservations, as well as to Petrified Forest National Park and the Painted Desert, but the city is a worthwhile destination in its own right. Set against a lovely backdrop of pine forests and the snowcapped San Francisco Peaks, Flagstaff is a laid-back college town with a frontier flavor.

In summer Phoenix residents head here seeking relief from the desert heat, because at any time of the year temperatures in Flagstaff are about 20°F cooler than in Phoenix. They also come to Flagstaff in winter to ski at the Arizona Snowbowl, about 15 miles northeast of town among the San Francisco Peaks.

GETTING HERE AND AROUND

Flagstaff lies at the intersection of I–40 (east–west) and I–17 (running south from Flagstaff), 146 miles north of Phoenix via I–17. If you're driving from Sedona to Flagstaff or the Grand Canyon, head north on U.S. 89A through the wooded Oak Creek Canyon: it's the most scenic route.

Flagstaff Airport is 3 miles south of town off I–17 at Exit 337. American flies from Phoenix to Flagstaff and offers a limited number of direct flights to Dallas. A taxi from Flagstaff Airport to downtown should cost about $15. Cabs aren't regulated; some, but not all, have meters, so it's wise to agree on a rate before you leave for your destination.

Amtrak comes into the downtown Flagstaff station twice daily. There's no rail service into Prescott or Sedona, but Groome

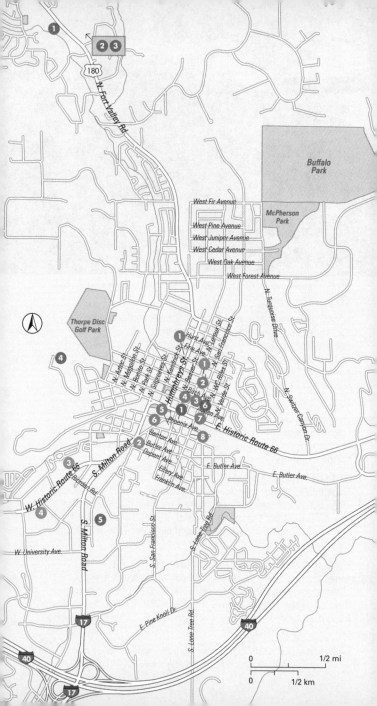

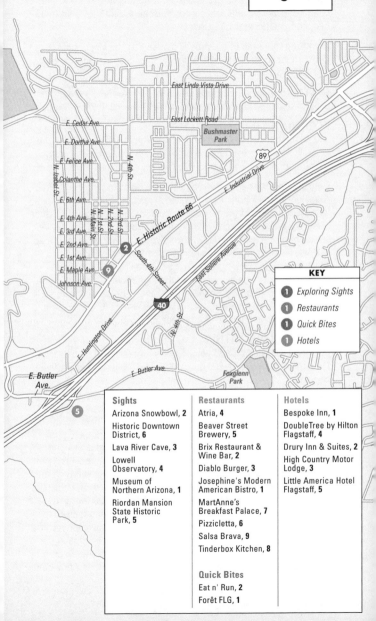

Flagstaff

KEY
- 1 Exploring Sights
- 1 Restaurants
- 1 Quick Bites
- 1 Hotels

Sights
Arizona Snowbowl, **2**
Historic Downtown District, **6**
Lava River Cave, **3**
Lowell Observatory, **4**
Museum of Northern Arizona, **1**
Riordan Mansion State Historic Park, **5**

Restaurants
Atria, **4**
Beaver Street Brewery, **5**
Brix Restaurant & Wine Bar, **2**
Diablo Burger, **3**
Josephine's Modern American Bistro, **1**
MartAnne's Breakfast Palace, **7**
Pizzicletta, **6**
Salsa Brava, **9**
Tinderbox Kitchen, **8**

Quick Bites
Eat n' Run, **2**
Forêt FLG, **1**

Hotels
Bespoke Inn, **1**
DoubleTree by Hilton Flagstaff, **4**
Drury Inn & Suites, **2**
High Country Motor Lodge, **3**
Little America Hotel Flagstaff, **5**

Transportation provides shuttle van service between Phoenix Sky Harbor Airport, Sedona, Camp Verde, Flagstaff, Tusayan, and the Grand Canyon. Several taxi companies can transport you around Flagstaff and northern Arizona.

A walking-tour map of the area is available at the visitor center in the Tudor Revival–style train depot, an excellent place to begin sightseeing.

CONTACTS Groome Transportation. ☎ *928/350–8466* ⊕ *www. groometransportation.com.* **Sun Taxi and Tours.** ☎ *928/774–7400.*

PLANNING YOUR TIME

You can see much of Flagstaff in a day—especially if you visit the Lowell Observatory in the evening—but plan an extra day or two for outdoor adventures and nearby Native American sites.

Consult the schedule of tour times if you want to visit the Riordan Mansion State Historic Park. Devote at least an hour to the excellent Museum of Northern Arizona. The Historic Downtown District is a great place for lunch or dinner and shopping. If you're a skier, spend part of a winter's day at the Arizona Snowbowl; in summer and fall, you can ride the chairlift for a fantastic view at nearly 11,000 feet. Take your time enjoying the trails on Mount Elden, and remember to pace yourself in the higher elevations. The Lava River Cave is an easy—if dark—hike that can be done comfortably in an hour; Walnut Canyon, where you can walk through ancient cliff dwellings, is only 20 minutes east of town.

VISITOR INFORMATION

CONTACT Flagstaff Visitor Center. ✉ *Santa Fe Depot, 1 E. Rte. 66, Downtown* ☎ *928/213–2951, 800/217–2367* ⊕ *www.flagstaffari-zona.org.*

 Sights

Arizona Snowbowl

VIEWPOINT | FAMILY | Although the Arizona Snowbowl is still one of Flagstaff's biggest attractions, snowy slopes can be a luxury in times of drought. Fortunately, visitors can enjoy the beauty of the area year-round, with or without the fluffy white stuff. The chairlift climbs the San Francisco Peaks to a height of 11,500 feet and doubles as a 30-minute scenic gondola ride in summer. From this vantage point you can see up to 70 miles; views may even include Sedona's red rocks and the Grand Canyon. There's a lodge at the base with a restaurant, bar, and ski school. To reach the ski area, take U.S. 180 north from Flagstaff; it's 7 miles from the Snowbowl

The tunnels of Lava River Cave were formed by lava flow hundreds of thousands of years ago.

exit to the sky-ride entrance. ✉ *9300 N. Snowbowl Rd., Grand Canyon* ☏ *928/447–9928* ⊕ *www.snowbowl.ski* ✉ *Varies.*

Historic Downtown District

HISTORIC DISTRICT | Storied Route 66 runs right through the heart of downtown Flagstaff. The late Victorian, Tudor Revival, and early art deco architecture in this district recalls the town's heyday as a logging and railroad center. The Santa Fe Depot now houses the visitor center. The 1927 Hotel Monte Vista, built after a community drive raised $200,000 in 60 days, is one of the art deco highlights of the district; today it houses a restaurant, live music venue, and a combination coffeehouse and cocktail bar. Across the street, the 1888 Babbitt Brothers Building was constructed as a building-supply store and then turned into a department store by David Babbitt, the mastermind of the Babbitt empire. (The Babbitts are one of Flagstaff's wealthiest founding families.) The Weatherford Hotel, built in 1900, hosted many celebrities; Western author Zane Grey wrote *The Call of the Canyon* here. Most of the area's first businesses were saloons catering to railroad construction workers, which was the case with the 1888 Vail Building. Nowadays, downtown is a bustling dining and retail district, with restaurants, bakeries, and alluring shops. Across the railroad tracks, the revitalized Southside is home to popular eateries and craft breweries. ✉ *Rte. 66 north to Birch Ave., and Beaver St. east to Agassiz St., Grand Canyon.*

Lava River Cave

CAVE | FAMILY | Subterranean lava flow formed this mile-long cave roughly 700,000 years ago. Once you descend into its boulder-strewn maw, the cave is spacious, with 40-foot ceilings, but claustrophobes take heed: about halfway through, the cave tapers to a 4-foot-high squeeze that can be a bit unnerving. A 40°F chill pervades the cave throughout the year so take warm clothing.

To reach the turnoff for the cave, go approximately 9 miles north of Flagstaff on U.S. 180, then turn west onto Forest Road (FR) 245. Turn left at the intersection of FR 171 and look for the sign to the cave. Note: these forest roads are closed from mid-November to March due to snow. The trip is approximately 45 minutes from Flagstaff. Although the cave is on Coconino National Forest Service property, there are no rangers on-site; the only thing here is an interpretive sign, so it's definitely something you tackle at your own risk. ■TIP→ **Pack a flashlight (or two).** ✉ *FR 171B, Grand Canyon* ⊕ *fs.usda.gov/coconino.*

★ Lowell Observatory

OBSERVATORY | FAMILY | In 1894 Boston businessman, author, and scientist Percival Lowell founded this observatory from which he studied Mars. His theories of the existence of a ninth planet sowed the seeds for the discovery of Pluto at Lowell in 1930 by Clyde Tombaugh. The 6,500-square-foot Steele Visitor Center hosts exhibits and lectures and has a stellar gift shop. Several interactive exhibits—among them Pluto Walk, a scale model of the solar system—appeal to children. Visitors can peer through several telescopes at the Giovale Open Deck Observatory, including the 24-inch Clark telescope and the McAllister, a 16-inch reflector telescope. ■TIP→ **The observatory is open and unheated, so dress for the outdoors.** ✉ *1400 W. Mars Hill Rd., Grand Canyon* ☎ *928/774–3358* ⊕ *www.lowell.edu* ✉ *From $29.*

Museum of Northern Arizona

HISTORY MUSEUM | FAMILY | This institution, founded in 1928, is respected worldwide for its research and for its collections centering on the natural and cultural history of the Colorado Plateau. Among the permanent exhibitions are an extensive collection of Navajo rugs and a Hopi *kiva* (men's ceremonial chamber).

A gallery devoted to area geology is usually a hit with children: it includes a life-size model dilophosaurus, a carnivorous dinosaur that once roamed northern Arizona. Outdoors a life-zone exhibit shows the changing vegetation from the bottom of the Grand Canyon to the highest peak in Flagstaff. A nature trail, open only in summer, heads down across a small stream into a canyon and up into an aspen grove. Also in summer the museum hosts exhibits

Side Trips Near Flagstaff

Travelers heading straight on toward the Grand Canyon often neglect the area north and east of Flagstaff, but a detour has its rewards. If you don't have time to do everything, take a quick drive to Walnut Canyon—it's only about 15 minutes out of town.

East of Flagstaff

Walnut Canyon National Monument consists of cliff dwellings constructed by the Sinagua people, who lived and farmed in and around the canyon starting around AD 700. The more than 300 dwellings here were built between 1080 and 1250 and abandoned around 1300. Early Flagstaff settlers looted the site for pots and "treasure"; Woodrow Wilson declared the site a national monument in 1915, which began a 30-year process of stabilizing the dwellings. Part of the fascination of Walnut Canyon is the opportunity to enter the dwellings, stepping back in time to an ancient way of life. Some of the Sinagua homes are in near-perfect condition in spite of all the looting, because of the dry, hot climate and the protection of overhanging cliffs. You can reach them by descending 185 feet on the 1-mile stepped Island Trail, which starts at the visitor center. As you follow the trail, look across the canyon for other dwellings not accessible on the path. Island Trail takes about an hour to complete at a normal pace. Those with health concerns should opt for the easier ½-mile Rim Trail, which has overlooks from which dwellings, as well as an excavated, reconstructed pit house, can be viewed. ⊕ *www. nps.gov/waca*.

Meteor Crater, a natural phenomenon in a privately owned park 43 miles east of Flagstaff, was created by a meteorite crash 49,000 years ago. A hole in the ground 600 feet deep, nearly a mile across, and more than 3 miles in circumference, Meteor Crater is large enough to accommodate the Washington Monument or 20 football fields. The area looks so much like the surface of the moon that NASA made it one of the official training sites for the Project Apollo astronauts. You can't descend into the crater because of the efforts of its owners to maintain its condition—scientists consider this to be the best-preserved crater on Earth—but guided rim tours, given every hour on the hour from 9 to 3, give useful background information. ⊕ *www.meteorcrater. com*.

San Francisco Volcanic Field

The **San Francisco Volcanic Field** north of Flagstaff encompasses 2,000 square miles of fascinating geological phenomena, including ancient volcanoes, cinder cones, valleys carved by water and ice, and the San Francisco Peaks themselves, some of which soar to almost 13,000 feet. There are also some of the most extensive Native American ruins in the Southwest. Both can be explored at Sunset Crater and Wupatki. Sunset Crater Volcano National Monument lies 14 miles northeast of Flagstaff off U.S. 89 and boasts a cinder cone, Sunset Crater, that rises 1,000 feet and was an active volcano 900 years ago. Because its final eruption contained iron and sulfur, the rim of the crater appears to glow. While you can walk around the base, you can't descend into the huge, fragile cone. The Lava Flow Trail, a mile-long self-guided walk, provides a good view of the evidence of the volcano's fiery power: lava formations and holes in the rock where volcanic gases vented to the surface.

Families from the Sinagua and other ancestral Puebloans are believed to have lived together in harmony on the site that is now **Wupatki National Monument**, farming and trading with one another and with those who passed through. The eruption of Sunset Crater may have influenced migration to this area a century after the event, as freshly laid volcanic cinders held in moisture needed for crops. Although there's evidence of earlier habitation, most of the settlers moved here around 1100 and left the pueblo by about 1250. The site for which the national monument was named, the Wupatki (meaning "tall house" in Hopi), was originally three stories high, built above an unexplored system of underground fissures. The structure had almost 100 rooms and an open ball court—evidence of Southwestern trade with Mesoamerican tribes for whom ball games were a central ritual. Other areas to visit are Wukoki, Lomaki, and the Citadel, a pueblo on a knoll above a limestone sink. Although the largest remnants of Native American settlements at Wupatki National Monument are open to the public, other sites are off-limits. If you're interested in an in-depth tour, consider a ranger-led overnight hike to the Crack-in-Rock Ruin. Conducted in April and October; the 14-mile round-trip trek covers areas marked by ancient petropyphs and dotted with well-preserved ruins. Between the Wupatki and Citadel ruins, the Doney Mountain affords 360-degree views of the Painted Desert and the San Francisco Volcanic Field.

and the works of Native American artists, whose wares are sold in the well-stocked museum gift shop. ⊠ *3101 N. Fort Valley Rd., Grand Canyon* ☎ *928/774–5213, 928/774–5211* ⊕ *musnaz.org* ⊡ *$15* ⊙ *Closed Tues.*

Riordan Mansion State Historic Park

HISTORIC HOME | This artifact of Flagstaff's logging heyday is near Northern Arizona University. The centerpiece is a mansion built in 1904 for Michael and Timothy Riordan, lumber-baron brothers who married two sisters. The 13,300-square-foot, 40-room log-and-stone structure—designed by Charles Whittlesley, who was also responsible for El Tovar Hotel at the Grand Canyon—contains furniture by Gustav Stickley, father of the American Arts and Crafts design movement. One room holds "Paul Bunyan's shoes," a two-foot-long pair of boots made by Timothy in his workshop. Everything on display is original to the house. The inside of the mansion may be explored only by guided tour (hourly on the hour); reservations are suggested. You can explore the exterior on a self-guided tour. ⊠ *409 W. Riordan Rd., Grand Canyon* ☎ *928/779–4395* ⊕ *www.azstateparks.com* ⊡ *$12 for guided tour* ⊙ *Closed Tues. and Wed. Nov.–Apr.*

 ## Restaurants

★ Atria

$$$$ | **AMERICAN** | Helmed by James Beard Award finalist Rochelle Daniel, this sleek downtown restaurant dazzles with a seasonal menu that is as much about presentation as it is about taste. Dine on fresh-caught fish, prime cuts of meat, and handmade pastas for dinner or share hot and cold appetizers—don't miss the roasted bone marrow—over cocktails or a glass of wine at the bar. **Known for:** beautifully plated dishes; eight-course tasting menu; creative cocktails and an impressive back bar. ⑤ *Average main: $40* ⊠ *103 N. Leroux St., Grand Canyon* ☎ *928/440–4377* ⊕ *www. atriarestaurant.com* ⊙ *Closed Sun. and Mon.*

Beaver Street Brewery

$$ | **AMERICAN** | **FAMILY** | This restaurant and microbrewery is a popular, casual, and family-friendly place with a pleasant patio. Wood-fired pizzas include the Enchanted Forest—with brie, portobello mushrooms, roasted red peppers, spinach, and artichoke pesto. **Known for:** crowd-pleasing pizza and pub fare; excellent craft beers; open until 10 p.m. Friday and Saturday. ⑤ *Average main: $19* ⊠ *11 S. Beaver St., Grand Canyon* ☎ *928/779–0079* ⊕ *beaverstreetbrewery.com.*

★ Brix Restaurant & Wine Bar

$$$$ | AMERICAN | A redbrick carriage house, built around 1910 as a garage for one of the first automobiles in Flagstaff, is home to one of the city's most sophisticated restaurants. With a seasonally updated menu, the chef pairs locally raised pork, beef, and roasted duck with wines from a list of almost 200 bottles (Brix refers to the sugar content of grapes at harvest). **Known for:** consistently delicious, locally sourced food; extensive wine list; commitment to sustainability. $ *Average main: $40 ⊠ 413 N. San Francisco St., Grand Canyon* ☎ *928/213–1021* ⊕ *www.brixflagstaff.com* ⊗ *Closed Sun. and Mon. No lunch.*

Diablo Burger

$$ | AMERICAN | With juicy burgers made from locally sourced, antibiotic- and hormone-free beef, this is arguably the best burger joint in the Southwest. Freshly cut fries lightly dusted with herbs, veggie burgers, grilled cheese sandwiches, and organic salads round out the menu. **Known for:** fantastic (and locally sourced) burgers; English muffin buns; crowds at lunchtime. $ *Average main: $15 ⊠ Heritage Square, 120 Leroux St., Grand Canyon* ☎ *928/774–3274* ⊕ *www.diabloburger.com.*

★ Josephine's Modern American Bistro

$$$$ | AMERICAN | Located in a Craftsman-style bungalow just a few blocks from Flagstaff's historic downtown, this fine-dining establishment serves bacon-wrapped filet mignon, braised short ribs, crab cakes, and smoked pork osso buco. The menu suggests wines from its extensive list to pair with each entrée, or you can order a craft cocktail from the creative bar. **Known for:** patio dining in summer; extensive, reasonably priced wine list; intimate, romantic atmosphere. $ *Average main: $32 ⊠ 503 N. Humphreys St., Grand Canyon* ☎ *928/779–3400* ⊕ *www.josephinesrestaurant. com* ⊗ *No dinner on Sun.*

MartAnne's Breakfast Palace

$$ | MEXICAN | FAMILY | Don't let the name mislead you: this South-of-the-border Route 66 diner serves breakfast (all day), lunch, and dinner in a bright space decorated with Día de Los Muertos–inspired paintings. House specialties include a green chile pork enchilada topped with two eggs and J.B.'s Volcano: a mound of chilaquiles drenched in that same green chile pork, loaded with chorizo and crowned by an over-medium egg. **Known for:** waits, especially on weekends, for breakfast; vibrantly colored walls and plates; generous portions. $ *Average main: $14 ⊠ 112 E. Rt. 66, Grand Canyon* ☎ *928/773–4701* ⊕ *martannes.com.*

Pizzicletta

$$ | ITALIAN | When you take your first bite of any one of the six expertly crafted pizzas on the menu—like the simple tomato, basil, and mozzarella, or the mascarpone, pecorino, arugula, and prosciutto—you'll understand why this small eatery has developed a fierce following. Plates of paper-thin cured meats and olives and salads with chèvre and pine nuts are equally delicious. **Known for:** elevating pizza-making to an art; homemade gelato; cool vibe. ⑤ *Average main: $17* ⊠ *203 W. Phoenix Ave., Grand Canyon* ☎ *928/774–3242* ⊕ *pizzicletta.com* ⊗ *No lunch Tues.–Fri.*

Salsa Brava

$$ | MEXICAN | FAMILY | This cheerful Mexican restaurant, with light-wood booths and colorful designs, eschews heavy Sonoran-style fare in favor of the grilled dishes found in Guadalajara. The fish tacos are particularly good, and you can substitute grilled vegetables for the rice and beans if you prefer a lower-carb meal. **Known for:** unpretentious, fresh Mexican food; plenty of gluten-free dishes; appearance on Food Network's Diners, Drive-Ins and Dives. ⑤ *Average main: $15* ⊠ *2220 E. Rte. 66, Grand Canyon* ☎ *928/779–5293* ⊕ *www.salsabravaflagstaff.com.*

Tinderbox Kitchen

$$$$ | MODERN AMERICAN | This deservedly popular downtown spot serves modern comfort food to local professionals and visiting foodies. Signature entrées include steelhead trout with jalapeño chimichurri, pineapple pork belly, and duck-leg confit. **Known for:** upscale, shareable comfort food; hip, sophisticated vibe; outstanding wine list. ⑤ *Average main: $35* ⊠ *34 S. San Francisco St., Grand Canyon* ☎ *928/226–8400* ⊕ *www.tinderboxkitchen.com* ⊗ *No lunch.*

Coffee and Quick Bites

Eat n' Run

$ | AMERICAN | Breakfast, lunch, and coffee on the run has risen to new heights with the presence of this friendly café on Route 66, a few miles east of downtown Flagstaff. Exceptional smoothies, breakfast burritos, and two avocado toast options, plus generous salads and sandwiches with house-made dressings and sauces accompany the coffee bar. **Known for:** great coffee; healthy (and delicious) breakfast and lunch; fast, friendly service. ⑤ *Average main: $11* ⊠ *2400 E. Rte 66, Grand Canyon* ☎ *928/679–9818* ⊕ *www.goodeatson66.com* ⊗ *Closed Sun. No dinner.*

Forêt FLG

$$ | **AMERICAN** | Upscale breakfast dishes like the *croque madame*—a grilled ham and fried egg sandwich drenched in cheesy mornay sauce—and Instagrammable coffee drinks and cocktails make this Southside coffee shop a good choice for a casual morning meal or brunch. On sunny days, sit on the patio and people-watch. **Known for:** patio dining; killer coffee and matcha drinks; breakfast options with a French twist. $ *Average main: $14* ⊠ *2 S. Beaver St., Suite 170, Grand Canyon* ☎ *928/214–7280* ⊕ *www.foretflagstaff.com* ☺ *Closed Mon. and Tues.*

Hotels

Trains pass through the downtown area along Route 66 about every 15 minutes throughout the day and night. Light sleepers may prefer to stay in the south or east section of town to avoid hearing trains rumbling through; at least the whistles are no longer blown within the downtown district.

★ Bespoke Inn

$$$$ | **B&B/INN** | This 1894 Craftsman-style historic property has nine luxuriously decorated rooms, some with fireplaces. **Pros:** plush bedding and linens; pet-friendly; within walking distance of downtown. **Cons:** breakfast is not offered; no elevator access to second floor; no completely ADA-compliant rooms. $ *Rooms from: $320* ⊠ *410 N. Leroux St., Grand Canyon* ☎ *844/259–7766, 928/981–4095* ⊕ *bespokeinnflagstaff.com* ⇆ *9 rooms* ⦿ *No Meals.*

DoubleTree by Hilton Flagstaff

$$ | **HOTEL** | This name-brand hotel on the west side of town is a good base for travelers heading to Williams to take the Grand Canyon Railway the next morning or explore Route 66 before driving to the South Rim or Grand Canyon West. **Pros:** no train noise; away from downtown traffic; on-site restaurant and cocktail lounge with fireplace. **Cons:** generic hotel without a lot of history; a drive to popular restaurants and attractions; hallways can be noisy. $ *Rooms from: $170* ⊠ *1175 W. Rte. 66, Grand Canyon* ☎ *855/610–8733, 928/773–8888* ⊕ *www.hilton.com* ⇆ *183 rooms* ⦿ *No Meals.*

Drury Inn & Suites

$$$ | **HOTEL** | So clean it sparkles, the Drury Inn sits at the edge of Northern Arizona University's campus and packs in the amenities, like happy-hour dinner and drinks, an indoor pool, and comfy lounge areas with mountain views. **Pros:** plenty of extras; great location (walk to campus and historic district); spacious and well-equipped rooms. **Cons:** large-scale property; generic-looking rooms; the parking garage is a bit of a trek. ⑤ *Rooms from: $215* ✉ *300 S. Milton Rd., Grand Canyon* ☎ *928/773–4900* ⊕ *www. druryhotels.com* ⇆ *160 rooms* ⦿ *Free Breakfast.*

High Country Motor Lodge

$$$ | MOTEL | With its hip, '60s vibe, this renovated motel attracts weary travelers and locals alike for live music, cocktails, and artisan pizzas at its on-site restaurant. **Pros:** cassette players (and cassettes) in each room; live music and movie nights; on-site Nordic spa. **Cons:** some noise from train and other rooms; sparse design with no microwave or desk; no early check-in. ⑤ *Rooms from: $200* ✉ *1000 W. Rte. 66, Grand Canyon* ☎ *866/928–4265, 928/774–5221* ⊕ *highcountrymotorlodge.com* ⇆ *123 rooms* ⦿ *No Meals.*

Little America Hotel Flagstaff

$$$ | HOTEL | FAMILY | This deservedly popular hotel is a little distance from the roar of the trains, the grounds are surrounded by evergreen forests, and it's one of the few places in Flagstaff with room service. **Pros:** large, clean rooms; many amenities, including restaurant, gym, pool, and store; walking trails through the forested grounds. **Cons:** large-scale property; a few miles east of the shopping and dining district; some highway noise outside (but rooms are quiet). ⑤ *Rooms from: $250* ✉ *2515 E. Butler Ave., Grand Canyon* ☎ *928/779–7900, 800/865–1401* ⊕ *flagstaff.littleamerica.com* ⇆ *247 rooms* ⦿ *No Meals.*

Nightlife

Flagstaff's large college contingent has plenty of places to gather after dark; most are in historic downtown and charge little or no cover. It's easy to walk from one rowdy spot to the next. The Flagstaff Brewery Trail (⊕ *craftbeerflg.com*) has six breweries within a 1-mile radius. During the summer months, catch free, family-friendly performances (music, theater, and dance) and movies Thursday to Saturday evenings outdoors at Heritage Square. For information on what's going on, pick up the free *Flagstaff Live.*

Annex Cocktail Lounge

COCKTAIL LOUNGES | The hip crowd here tends to be postcollege and more affluent; the cocktails are creative, the food is great, and there's often live music on the wraparound patio. ✉ *50 S. San Francisco St., Grand Canyon* ☎ *928/774–2811* ⊕ *www.annexcocktaillounge.com.*

Collins Irish Pub & Grill
BARS | DJs spin high-energy tunes as a mostly college-age crowd takes to the dance floor Thursday, Friday, and Saturday nights from 10 pm until close. ✉ *2 N. Leroux St., Grand Canyon* ☎ *928/214–7363.*

Mountain Top Tap Room
LIVE MUSIC | This 36-tap watering hole on Route 66 hosts open mic and karaoke nights plus the occasional band on weekends. ✉ *10 E. Rte. 66, Grand Canyon* ☎ *320/339–8593* ⊕ *www.mountain-toptaproom.com* ☉ *Closed Tues.*

Museum Club Roadhouse and Danceclub
LIVE MUSIC | Fondly known as the Zoo, this Flagstaff institution once housed an extensive taxidermy collection in the 1930s and is now a popular country-and-western club (a few owls still perch above the dance floor). A gigantic log cabin constructed around five trees, with a huge, wishbone-shape pine as the entryway, the venue offers a taste of Route 66 color along with live music and other events. ✉ *3404 E. Rte. 66, Grand Canyon* ☎ *928/440–4331* ⊕ *www.museumclub.net.*

Rendezvous
LIVE MUSIC | This lounge in the historic Hotel Monte Vista packs 'em in three nights a week with live blues, jazz, classic rock, and punk. ✉ *Hotel Monte Vista, 100 N. San Francisco St., Grand Canyon* ☎ *928/440–7771* ⊕ *www.hotelmontevista.com.*

Weatherford Hotel
LIVE MUSIC | You'll find three bars here: Charly's Pub & Grill hosts late-night jazz and blues bands, while, in the basement, the Gopher Hole has a game room and brings a mix of styles to its stage. The third, the Zane Grey Ballroom upstairs, affords a great view of the city you can enjoy with your drink. Good food and historical charm enhance the experience. ✉ *23 N. Leroux St., Grand Canyon* ☎ *928/779–1919* ⊕ *weatherfordhotel.com.*

 Performing Arts

Coconino Center for the Arts
ARTS CENTERS | Many excellent art exhibitions, theatrical productions, and music performances take place at Coconino Center for the Arts under the direction of Creative Flagstaff. ✉ *2300 N. Fort Valley Rd., Grand Canyon* ☎ *928/779–2300* ⊕ *www.ccaflagstaff.org.*

Flagstaff Symphony Orchestra

MUSIC | Classical concerts from September to April, mostly held in Ardrey Auditorium on the NAU campus, are given by the Flagstaff Symphony Orchestra. ⊠ *Grand Canyon* ☎ *928/774–5107* ⊕ *www. flagstaffsymphony.org.*

Orpheum Theater

CONCERTS | The 1917 Orpheum Theater, in the heart of the historic district, features music acts, films, lectures, and plays. ⊠ *15 W. Aspen Ave., Grand Canyon* ☎ *928/556–1580* ⊕ *www.orpheumflag-staff.com.*

Theatrikos Theatre Company

THEATER | This highly regarded performance-art group produces five mainstage productions annually using a diverse base of local talent. ⊠ *11 W. Cherry Ave., Grand Canyon* ☎ *928/774–1662* ⊕ *theatrikos.com.*

Shopping

The Artists' Gallery

CRAFTS | For fine arts and crafts—everything from ceramics and stained glass to weaving and painting—visit the Artists' Gallery, a local artists' cooperative. ⊠ *17 N. San Francisco St., Grand Canyon* ☎ *928/773–0958* ⊕ *theflagstaffartistsgallery.com.*

Babbitt's Backcountry Outfitters

SPORTING GOODS | Just about all your sporting-goods needs can be met here. ⊠ *12 E. Aspen Ave., Grand Canyon* ☎ *928/774–4775* ⊕ *babbittsbackcountry.com.*

Bookmans

BOOKS | Packed solid with used books, music, musical instruments, and movies, Bookmans is also a laid-back café where you can munch on pastries, surf the Internet, and hear live folk music. ⊠ *1520 S. Riordan Ranch St., Grand Canyon* ☎ *928/774–0005* ⊕ *bookmans.com.*

Flagstaff General Store

SOUVENIRS | A mix of home decor, vintage goods, and crafts made by more than 35 local artists fills the rooms at this eclectic shop. ⊠ *9 N. Leroux St., Grand Canyon* ☎ *928/225–2057* ⊕ *flagstaffgen-eralstore.com.*

Museum of Northern Arizona Gift Shop

SOUVENIRS | High-quality Native American art, jewelry, and crafts can be found here. ⊠ *3101 N. Fort Valley Rd., Grand Canyon* ☎ *928/774–5213* ⊕ *musnaz.org* ☉ *Closed Tues.*

Peace Surplus

SPORTING GOODS | In addition to selling everything from hiking boots to MREs (meals ready to eat), this sporting goods store rents tents, sleeping bags, backpacks, and ski equipment. ⊠ *14 W. Rte. 66, Grand Canyon* ☎ *928/779–4521* ⊕ *peacesurplus.com.*

Winter Sun Trading Company

SOUVENIRS | This company sells medicinal herbs, unique fragrances, and Native American jewelry and crafts. ⊠ *107 N. San Francisco St., Suite 1, Grand Canyon* ☎ *928/774–2884* ⊕ *www. wintersun.com.*

Activities

HIKING

You can explore Arizona's alpine tundra in the San Francisco Peaks, part of the Coconino National Forest, where more than 80 species of plants grow on the upper elevations. The habitat is fragile, so hikers are asked to stay on established trails (there are lots of them).

■ **TIP→ Flatlanders should give themselves a day or two to adjust to the altitude before lengthy or strenuous hiking.**

The altitude here will make even the hardiest hikers breathe a little harder, so anyone with cardiac or respiratory problems should be cautious about overexertion. Note that most of the forest trails aren't accessible during winter due to snow.

Coconino National Forest–Flagstaff Ranger District

HIKING & WALKING | The rangers of the Coconino National Forest maintain many of the region's trails and can provide you with details on hiking in the area. Excellent maps of the Flagstaff trails are sold here for $14. Both the forest's main office in West Flagstaff and the ranger station in East Flagstaff (⊠ *5075 N. U.S. 89*) are open weekdays 8–4. ⊠ *1824 S. Thompson St., Grand Canyon* ☎ *928/527–3600 for main office, West Flagstaff, 928/526–0866 for East Flagstaff office* ⊕ *fs.usda.gov/coconino.*

Elden Lookout Trail

HIKING & WALKING | The most challenging trail in the Mount Elden trail system, which happens to be the route with the most rewarding views, is along the steep switchbacks of the Elden Lookout Trail. If you traverse the full 3 miles to the top, keep your focus on the landscape rather than the tangle of antennae and satellite dishes that greets you at the end. *Difficult.* ⊠ *Grand Canyon* ⊹ *Trailhead: off U.S. 89, 3 miles east of downtown Flagstaff.*

★ Humphreys Peak Trail

HIKING & WALKING | Climbing Arizona's highest peak is on many a hiker's bucket list, and this 10-mile round-trip to the 12,600-foot summit will satisfy and delight experienced hikers. You'll travel the first few miles through meadows and pine forest; then it's a rocky, steep ascent to the top, where 360-degree views of the Grand Canyon, the Painted Desert, and the Verde Valley await. Beware of the thin air at this altitude—the trail starts at 8,800 feet—and set aside a whole day. *Difficult.* ⊠ *Trailhead: North end of Snowbowl's lower parking lot; Snowbowl Rd., off U.S. 180., Grand Canyon.*

Kachina Trail

HIKING & WALKING | Those who don't want a long hike can do just the first mile or two of the 5-mile-long Kachina Trail; gently rolling, this route is surrounded by huge stands of aspen and offers fantastic vistas. In fall, changing leaves paint the landscape shades of yellow, russet, and amber. *Moderate.* ⊠ *Grand Canyon ⊹ Trailhead: Snowbowl Rd., 7 miles north of U.S. 180.*

Sunset Trail

HIKING & WALKING | The 4-mile-long Sunset Trail proceeds with a gradual pitch through the pine forest, emerging onto a narrow ridge nicknamed the Catwalk. By all means take pictures of the stunning valley views, but make sure your feet are well placed. The access road to this trail is closed in winter. *Moderate.* ⊠ *Off U.S. 180, 3 miles north of downtown Flagstaff, then 6 miles east on FR 420/Schultz Pass Rd., Grand Canyon.*

HORSEBACK RIDING

AZ High Mountain Trail Rides at Mormon Lake

HORSEBACK RIDING | Ride through the ponderosa pine forests near Mormon Lake, just southeast of Flagstaff, on 30-, 60-, and 90-minute trail rides May through September. The two-hour Lake View ride combines parts of the other trails. The stable also gives horse-drawn wagon rides through Mormon Lake Village. ⊠ *2040 Mormon Lake Rd., Grand Canyon* ☎ *928/354–2359* ⊕ *highmountaintrailrides.com.*

Hitchin' Post Stables

HORSEBACK RIDING | The wranglers at Hitchin' Post Stables lead rides through ponderosa pine and stop for scenic photographs of Western wagons. Longer two- and three-hour rides continue to the mouth of Walnut Canyon. ⊠ *4848 Lake Mary Rd., Grand Canyon* ☎ *928/774–1719* ⊕ *historichitchinpoststables.com* 🛒 *$80 for 1-hr ride.*

MOUNTAIN BIKING

With more than 50 miles of urban bicycle trails and more than 30 miles of challenging forest and mountain trails a short ride from town, it was inevitable that one of Flagstaff's best-kept secrets would leak out. The mountain bicycling on Mount Elden is on par with that of more celebrated trails in Colorado and Utah. Although there isn't a concise loop trail such as those in Moab, Utah, experienced bicyclers can create one by connecting Schultz Creek Trail, Sunset Trail, and Elden Lookout Road. Beginners (as well as those looking for rewarding scenery with less of an incline) may want to start with Lower Fort Valley and Campbell Mesa. Local bicycle-shop staff can help with advice and planning. Pick up a FUTS (Flagstaff Urban Trails System) map at the visitor center detailing low- and no-traffic bicycle routes around town.

Arizona Nordic Village

BIKING | From mid-June through mid-October, the Arizona Nordic Village opens its cross-country trails for mountain bicycling—good for families and beginners because they're scenic and not technically challenging. During winter you can rent snow bikes here. ⊠ 16848 U.S. 180, Grand Canyon ✛ 16 miles north of Flagstaff ☎ 928/220–0550 ⊕ www.arizonanordicvillage.com.

★ Lower Oldham Trail

BIKING | Originating on the north end of Buffalo Park in Flagstaff, the Lower Oldham Trail is steep in some sections but rewarding. The terrain rolls, climbing about 800 feet in 3 miles, and the trail is difficult in spots but easy enough to test your tolerance of the elevation. Many fun trails spur off this one; it's best to stop in at the local bicycle shop to get trail maps and discuss rides with staff who know the area. ⊠ Grand Canyon ✛ Trailhead: Buffalo Park, 2400 N. Gemini Rd.

Schultz Creek Trail

BIKING | The popular Schultz Creek Trail is fun and suitable for strong beginners, although seasoned experts will be thrilled as well. Most opt to start at the top of the 600-foot-high hill and swoop down the smooth, twisting path through groves of wildflowers and stands of ponderosa pines and aspens, ending at the trailhead four giddy miles later. ⊠ Grand Canyon ✛ Trailhead: Schultz Pass Rd., near intersection with U.S. 180.

EQUIPMENT AND RENTALS
Absolute Bikes

BIKING | You can rent mountain bicycles, get good advice and gear, and purchase trail maps here. ⊠ 202 E. Rte. 66, Grand Canyon ☎ 928/779–5969 ⊕ www.absolutebikes.net.

Flagstaff Bike Revolution

BIKING | This shop rents, sells, and repairs bicycles south of the tracks, next door to Mother Road Brewing Company. ⊠ *3 S. Mikes Pike, Grand Canyon* ☎ *928/774–3042* ⊕ *flagbikerev.com.*

ROCK CLIMBING

Flagstaff Climbing Center

ROCK CLIMBING | The tallest indoor climbing walls in the Southwest can be found at this rock-climbing gym and its second location on Main Street. ⊠ *205 S. San Francisco St., Grand Canyon* ☎ *928/556–9909* ⊕ *flagstaffclimbing.com.*

SKIING AND SNOWBOARDING

The ski season usually starts in mid-December and ends in mid-April.

Arizona Nordic Village

SKIING & SNOWBOARDING | **FAMILY** | Nine miles north of Snowbowl Road, the Flagstaff Nordic Center has 25 miles of well-groomed cross-country trails for cross-country skiing and snowshoeing that are open daily (when there's enough snow). Coffee, hot chocolate, and snacks are served at the lodge. Equipment rental and snow bikes ("fat tires") are available as full-day or half-day packages. ⊠ *16848 U.S. 180, Grand Canyon* ✛ *16 miles north of Flagstaff* ☎ *928/220–0550* ⊕ *www.arizonanordicvillage.com.*

Arizona Snowbowl

SKIING & SNOWBOARDING | **FAMILY** | Fourteen miles north of Flagstaff off U.S. 180, the Arizona Snowbowl, on the western slope of Humphreys Peak, has 55 downhill runs, eight lifts, and a vertical drop of 2,800 feet. The eight-person Agassiz Lift gondolas whisk skiers 2,000 feet up in seven minutes, affording a fabulous view of the Grand Canyon in the distance. There are three restaurants, an equipment-rental and retail shop, and a SkiWee center for kids ages four to seven.

All-day adult lift tickets are $99, and children 10 and under can ski for free all season. (Prices can vary based on dates and demand.) The closest lodging to the ski area is Basecamp Lodge, with cabins and a restaurant at the base of the mountain. Some Flagstaff motels have ski packages that include transportation to Snowbowl. ⊠ *Snowbowl Rd., Grand Canyon* ☎ *928/447–9928* ⊕ *www.snowbowl.ski.*

TOURS

Ventures

ADVENTURE TOURS | The Ventures program, run by the education department of the Museum of Northern Arizona, offers day trips and multiday tours of the area led by local scientists, artists, and historians. Trips might include rafting excursions down the San Juan River, treks into the Grand Canyon or Colorado Plateau backcountry, or bus tours into the Navajo Reservation to visit with Native American artists. Prices start at about $100 for day trips and go up to $1,500 for outdoor adventures. ⊠ *Grand Canyon* ☎ *928/774–5211* ⊕ *musnaz.org/travel* ⌕ *From $100.*

Williams

59 miles south of Grand Canyon National Park, 36 miles west of Flagstaff.

If you are heading to the Grand Canyon from points west, Williams makes sense as a base, especially if you want to take the Grand Canyon Railway. The mountain town encompasses a nicely preserved ½ mile of Route 66, originally built to accommodate adventurous cross-country motorists. Sure, there are kitschy 1950s diners and souvenir shops, along with cowboys who enact staged gunfights behind the train depot, but you'll also find good restaurants, charming lodging, a few microbreweries, and outdoor activities like hiking, biking, and fishing.

GETTING HERE AND AROUND
From Flagstaff, you can take Exit 165 to reach the historic downtown area. You'll end up on Railroad Avenue, the one-way westbound street. If you're coming from points west, take Exit 163, Grand Canyon Boulevard, into the heart of town. Most shops and restaurants are along Route 66 (also called Main Street) and Railroad Avenue, which runs parallel. The Williams Visitor Center is on the corner of Railroad Avenue and Grand Canyon Boulevard, and there's a free parking lot next to it. The Grand Canyon Railway Depot is across the tracks.

VISITOR INFORMATION
CONTACT Williams Visitor Center. ⊠ *200 W. Railroad Ave. at Grand Canyon Blvd., Williams* ☎ *928/635–4061* ⊕ *www.experiencewilliams.com.*

 Sights

Bearizona Wildlife Park
WILDLIFE REFUGE | FAMILY | Drive through 3 miles of ponderosa pine forest in this wildlife park to observe black bears up close in their natural environment, all from the comfort of your car. You can also walk through a zoo setting to see animals including otters, beavers, reindeer, porcupines, wolves, and bobcats, more than

At the Grand Canyon you can get up close and personal with adorable baby deer.

half of which were rescued. It's a good stop for families who need a detour on the way to the Grand Canyon's South Rim, one hour away. ✉ *1500 E. Rte. 66, Grand Canyon* ☎ *928/635–2289* ⊕ *bearizona.com* ✉ *$25 for children on weekends, $35 for adults on weekends ($20, $30 on weekdays).*

Grand Canyon Deer Farm

FARM/RANCH | FAMILY | You can feed deer raised from babies, walk with wallabies, and pet llamas on this 10-acre animal farm near Williams. The farm also has coatimundi, bison, peacocks, goats, camels, and more. True animal lovers can book an interactive experience with some of the farm's inhabitants for an additional fee. ✉ *6769 E. Deer Farm Rd., Grand Canyon* ☎ *928/635–4073* ⊕ *deerfarm.com* ✉ *$16.*

🍴 Restaurants

Cruisers Café 66

$$ | AMERICAN | FAMILY | Patterned after a '50s-style high-school hangout (but with cocktail service), this diner pleases kids and adults with a large menu of family-priced American classics— good burgers and fries, barbecue pork sandwiches, salads, and mesquite-smoked ribs. A large mural of the town's heyday along the "Mother Road" and a historic car on the roof make this a Route 66 favorite. **Known for:** burgers and barbecue; nice patio; craft beers from local breweries. ⑤ *Average main: $20* ✉ *233 W. Rte. 66, Grand Canyon* ☎ *928/635–2445* ⊕ *www.cruisers66.com.*

Dara Thai Twisters

$ | **ASIAN** | **FAMILY** | Formerly a popular diner and soda fountain known as Twisters, this Thai restaurant serves curries, noodle dishes, and tom yum soup. Sip beer or tiger milk tea, a form of boba, and finish with a scoop of ice cream surrounded by Route 66 nostalgia. **Known for:** Thai food served in a '50s-style diner; vegetarian options; tiger milk tea. ⑤ *Average main: $9* ⊠ *417 E. Rte. 66, Grand Canyon* ☎ *928/635–0266* ⊗ *Closed Sun.*

Pine Country Restaurant

$$ | **DINER** | **FAMILY** | Faux pine boughs, pine dining booths, and curtains that only a grandma would hang lend a country charm to this diner known for its extra-large pies and downhome country cooking. Breakfast lovers dig into homemade cinnamon rolls, huevos rancheros with pork green chile, and omelets, while later in the day sandwiches, steaks, ribs, salads, and pastas dominate the menu. **Known for:** fresh-baked pies, stuffed with decadent fillings; coffee bar with drinks named for famous cowboys; traditional and Mexican breakfasts served all day. ⑤ *Average main: $19* ⊠ *107 N. Grand Canyon Blvd., Grand Canyon* ☎ *928/635–9718* ⊕ *pinecountryrestaurant.com.*

★ Red Raven Restaurant

$$$ | **ECLECTIC** | This dapper bistro in the heart of downtown Williams, with warm lighting and romantic booth seating, blends American, Italian, and Asian ingredients into creative and delicious fare. Specialties include a starter of crisp tempura shrimp salad with house-made cocktail sauce and mains like charbroiled salmon with basil butter over cranberry–pine nut couscous. **Known for:** upscale dining in Williams; good wine list; continental and Italian specialties. ⑤ *Average main: $28* ⊠ *135 W. Rte. 66, Grand Canyon* ☎ *928/635–4980* ⊕ *www.redravenrestaurant.com* ⊗ *Closed Sun.*

 Hotels

Canyon Motel and RV Park

$ | **HOTEL** | **FAMILY** | Sleep in a historic railcar or a stone cottage from a 1938 motor lodge at this 13-acre property at the forest's edge on the outskirts of Williams. **Pros:** family-friendly property with train cars, horseshoes, playground, and indoor swimming pool; general store; friendly and helpful owners. **Cons:** short drive to restaurants and shops; RV-park traffic; rate for train car rooms much higher. ⑤ *Rooms from: $107* ⊠ *1900 E. Rodeo Rd., Rte. 66, Grand Canyon* ☎ *928/635–9371* ⊕ *www.thecanyonmotel.com* ⇆ *23 units* ⦿ *No Meals.*

Grand Canyon Railway Hotel

$$$ | **HOTEL** | **FAMILY** | Designed to resemble the train depot's original Fray Marcos Hotel, this upscale place features attractive Southwestern-style accommodations with large bathrooms and comfy beds with upscale linens. **Pros:** railway package options and convenience; indoor pool and outdoor playground; short walk from historic downtown restaurants and bars. **Cons:** large-scale property; pricey for these parts; pets must be boarded at on-site kennel. *$ Rooms from: $250 ⊠ 235 N. Grand Canyon Blvd., Grand Canyon ☎ 928/635–4010, 800/843–8724 ⊕ www.thetrain.com ⮑ 298 rooms ❍❍ No Meals.*

The Red Garter

$$ | **B&B/INN** | This restored saloon and bordello from 1897 now houses a small, antiques-filled B&B. **Pros:** on-site coffeehouse and café; decorated in antiques and period pieces; steps from several restaurants and bars. **Cons:** all rooms are accessible only by stairs; parking is across the street; no children under eight. *$ Rooms from: $165 ⊠ 137 Railroad Ave., Grand Canyon ☎ 928/635–1484, 800/328–1484 ⊕ www.redgarter.com ⮑ 4 rooms ❍❍ No Meals.*

★ Sheridan House Inn

$$$$ | **B&B/INN** | Nestled among two acres of pine trees a ½ mile uphill from Route 66, this upscale B&B has decks with good views and a flagstone patio with a hot tub. **Pros:** quiet location; scrumptious breakfasts; warm, helpful hosts. **Cons:** must drive to downtown Williams, where parking is scarce; no children under 16; some rooms are upstairs (no elevator). *$ Rooms from: $320 ⊠ 460 E. Sheridan Ave., Grand Canyon ☎ 928/635–8991 ⊕ www. sheridanhouseinn.com ⮑ 8 rooms ❍❍ Free Breakfast.*

Nightlife

Grand Canyon Wine Co.

WINE BARS | This cozy wine bar on Route 66 pours Arizona wines by the glass or as part of a flight. You can also purchase a bottle to share with friends or sample tapped beers made by neighboring Historic Brewing Company. Even though the bar doesn't have its own kitchen, it does have a menu featuring pizzas and Caesar salad from its sister restaurant, Station 66, next door. ⊠ *138 W. Rte. 66, Grand Canyon ☎ 855/598–0999 ⊕ grandcanyonwineco.com.*

Shopping

Addicted to Route 66

SOUVENIRS | Home to the world's largest Route 66 shield sign— look for it on the back wall—this store is nirvana for Mother

Road enthusiasts. Buy T-shirts, '50s-theme art and posters, and Route 66 memorabilia. ⊠ *124 W. Rte. 66, Grand Canyon* ☎ *928/635–5229.*

★ Colors of the West

SOUVENIRS | The largest gift shop in Willliams, Colors of the West has more than 300 T-shirt designs, 100 different hot sauces, and 90 styles of coffee mugs, plus everything from decorative wind chimes to a whole row of Christmas ornaments. ⊠ *201 W. Rte. 66, Grand Canyon* ☎ *928/635–9559* ⊕ *colorsofthewestusa.com.*

Thunder Eagle

JEWELRY & WATCHES | Specializing in high-quality Native American jewelry and art, this store offers one of the largest selections in the state of pieces certified by the Council for Indigenous Art and Culture. ⊠ *221 W. Rte. 66, Grand Canyon* ☎ *928/635–8889.*

 ## Activities

Canyon Coaster Adventure Park

AMUSEMENT PARK/CARNIVAL | Home to Arizona's only mountain coaster, this adventure park attracts thrill seekers year-round to tube on fresh snow in the winter and mountain tube on specially designed tracks in the summer. The open-air coaster twists, turns, and corkscrews through the pines as you control its speed up to 27 miles per hour. ⊠ *700 E. Rte. 66, Grand Canyon* ☎ *928/707–7729* ⊕ *canyoncoasteradventurepark.com* ⊠ *$20 per ride on coaster.*

Devil Dog Loop Trail

BIKING | Cyclists can enjoy the scenery along abandoned sections of Route 66 on this easy 5-mile trail. Maps of mountain bike trails are available at the Williams Visitor Center or on the Kaibab National Forest website. ⊠ *Grand Canyon* ⊕ *www.fs.usda.gov/kaibab.*

Cameron

25 miles southwest of Tuba City on U.S. 89.

Cameron Trading Post and Motel, established in 1916 and overlooking a spectacular gorge and vintage suspension bridge, is one of the few remaining authentic trading posts in the Southwest. It's a convenient stop if you're driving to the Grand Canyon and has reasonably priced dining, lodging, camping, and shopping. The community around it has a gas station, restaurants, and shops for souvenirs and Native American crafts.

GETTING HERE AND AROUND

Cameron and the historic trading post are along the main highway (U.S. 89) between Flagstaff and Page and just 30 miles from the eastern entrance to the South Rim of the Grand Canyon.

Restaurants

Blue Canyon Grill

$ | **AMERICAN** | In addition to Navajo tacos, this local favorite plates breakfast burritos in the morning and smoked ribs, fried chicken, and sandwiches later in the day. It's no frills but reliable and budget-friendly. **Known for:** local hangout; cheap eats; menu printed on a blackboard. ⑤ *Average main: $9* ✉ *465 Hwy. 89, Grand Canyon* ☎ *928/679–2455.*

Grand Canyon Restaurant & Dining

$$ | **AMERICAN** | At this restaurant inside the Cameron Trading post, you can sample Native American specialties including Navajo tacos made with fry bread and ground beef, Navajo burgers served with fry bread instead of a bun, and Navajo beef stew accompanied by—you guessed it—fry bread. Sandwiches, Mexican favorites, and entrées off the grill round out the menu. **Known for:** fry bread; Mexican breakfasts; one of the few restaurants in the area. ⑤ *Average main: $15* ✉ *466 U.S. 89, Grand Canyon* ☎ *800/338–7385, 928/679–2231* ⊕ *www.camerontradingpost. com.*

🛏 Hotels

Cameron Trading Post

$$ | **HOTEL** | At the turnoff for the western entrance to the Grand Canyon's South Rim, this trading post dates back to 1916 and contains recently renovated Southwestern-style rooms with carved-oak furniture, tile baths, and balconies overlooking the Colorado River. **Pros:** impressive collection of Southwestern art; restaurant serving Native American specialties; historic lodging with campground next door. **Cons:** high traffic volume; occasional highway noise; somewhat remote. ⑤ *Rooms from: $150* ✉ *466 U.S. 89, Grand Canyon* ☎ *800/338–7385* ⊕ *www.camerontradingpost.com* ⇥ *66 rooms* ⦿ *No Meals.*

👜 Shopping

★ Cameron Trading Post

SOUVENIRS | An authentic trading post, this massive stop has all the typical Native American arts and crafts you'd expect—jewelry,

Did You Know?

The Cameron Trading Post in the town of Cameron, Arizona, is one of the few remaining authentic trading posts in the Southwest. It was founded in 1916 by brothers C.D. and Hubert Richardson. In the early days Navajo and Hopi locals would barter their wool, blankets, and livestock for dry goods.

rugs, pottery, even sand paintings—but it also has items you're not likely to see elsewhere, such as Navajo-inspired cross-stitch kits and prickly pear honey. ✉ *466 Hwy. 89, Grand Canyon* ☎ *800/338–7385, 928/679–2231* ⊕ *www.camerontradingpost. com.*

Navajo Trail Trading Post

SOUVENIRS | Inside the Chevron station, this gift shop sells Native American jewelry, dream catchers, T-shirts, and Tony Hillerman books. There are also a McAlister's Deli and a Burger King here. ✉ *Grand Canyon* ✛ *Intersection of U.S. 89 and Hwy. 64* ☎ *928/697–3631* ⊕ *navajotrailtradingpost.com.*

Lees Ferry

85 miles from the North Rim entrance via Hwy. 89A to Hwy. 67.

En route from the South Rim to the North Rim and about 5 miles northeast of the town of Marble Canyon, where Echo Cliffs and Vermilion Cliffs intersect, is Lees Ferry. Considered "mile zero" of the river—the point from which all distances on the rivers system in the Grand Canyon are measured—Lees Ferry is where most of the Grand Canyon river rafts put into the water. Huge trout lurk in the river near here, and there are several places in the area to pick up angling gear and a guide.

Other than Lees Ferry, there isn't another vehicle crossing point on the Colorado River until the Glen Canyon Dam Bridge near Hoover Dam (although two footbridges cross the river near Phantom Ranch). Lees Ferry, at the Pariah Canyon junction just 15 miles below Glen Canyon Dam, has for thousands of years offered one of the best places to cross the deep gash of the Grand Canyon. Today the town—including the Lonely Dell Ranch Historic District, a small, sad cemetery, and a scattering of historic buildings—offers a glimpse of frontier life. But most people journey to Lees Ferry to get onto the river. Commercial raft trips take off from the boat ramps, and fly-fishing guides regularly shuttle people upstream to the base of Glen Canyon Dam.

 Sights

Lonely Dell Ranch Historic Site

FARM/RANCH | A 1-mile round-trip self-guided walk takes visitors past homestead buildings and an orchard left by early Mormon missionaries. ✉ *Grand Canyon* ⊕ *www.nps.gov/places/lonely-dell-ranch-historic-site.htm.*

Walk across the Glen Canyon Dam Bridge, a stunning steel-arch structure spanning the Colorado River, to snap a few photos of the dam and Lake Powell.

 Activities

CAMPING

Lees Ferry Campground

CAMPGROUND | Situated on a mesa overlooking the Colorado River, this campground has 54 designed sites, modern bathrooms, and an RV dump station. Reservations are not accepted. ⊠ *Lees Ferry, Grand Canyon.*

HIKING

Cathedral Wash Trail

HIKING & WALKING | This 3-mile out-and-back trail snakes through a canyon and ends at the Colorado River. Some scrambling is required, and at times there is no marked trail over the rocks. ⊠ *Grand Canyon.*

Spencer Trail

HIKING & WALKING | This strenuous, 4-mile trek involves a steep climb with seven switchbacks, narrow squeezes, and loose rock, but it rewards with views of Glen Canyon and the Colorado River. ⊠ *Grand Canyon.*

Jacob Lake

42 miles from the North Rim entrance via Hwy. 67.

The tiny town of Jacob Lake, nestled high in pine country at an elevation of 7,925 feet, was named after Mormon explorer Jacob Hamblin, also known as the Buckskin Missionary. It has a hotel, café, and campground, and it makes a good base for exploring the beautiful Kaibab Plateau.

VISITOR INFORMATION

Kaibab Plateau Visitor Center

VISITOR CENTER | The U.S. Forest Service's Kaibab Plateau Visitor Center is open May through mid-October and has several interpretive displays, books, and educational gifts. Gas and groceries are available next door at Jacob Lake Inn. ⊠ *U.S. 89A and Hwy. 67, Jacob Lake* ☎ *928/643–7298* ⊕ *www.fs.usda.gov/recarea/kaibab.*

Restaurants

Jacob Lake Inn Restaurant

$$ | **AMERICAN** | This restaurant inside Jacob Lake Inn satisfies hungry travelers with homemade breakfasts and burgers and sandwiches for lunch. At dinnertime, try the grilled Salisbury steak topped with grilled onions; add hunter gravy and an egg to enjoy it like a local. Or, sample a regional trout dish. **Known for:** homemade pies; Navajo rugs and sandpaintings on the wall; counter seating. ⑤ *Average main: $14* ⊠ *U.S. 89A & Hwy. 67, Grand Canyon* ☎ *928/643–7232* ⊕ *www.jacoblake.com.*

Hotels

Jacob Lake Inn

$$ | **HOTEL** | The bustling lodge at Jacob Lake Inn is a popular stop for those heading to the North Rim, 45 miles south. **Pros:** grocery store, bakery, and restaurant; quiet rooms; good base for exploring North Rim. **Cons:** only the newer rooms have TVs; no Internet; cabin rooms don't have air-conditioning. ⑤ *Rooms from: $155* ⊠ *U.S. 89A and Hwy. 67, Grand Canyon* ☎ *928/643–7232* ⊕ *www. jacoblake.com* ⇆ *58 rooms* ⑩ *No Meals.*

Kaibab Lodge

$$ | **HOTEL** | Built in 1926, this lodge sits on the edge of a meadow just 5 miles from the national park's entrance. **Pros:** historic property; just a few miles from the park's boundary; meadow views. **Cons:** no air-conditioning; paper-thin walls; no TV or Wi-Fi. ⑤ *Rooms* *from: $150* ✉ *Grand Canyon* ☎ *928/638–2389* ⊕ *kaibablodge.com* ⊗ *Closed mid-Oct.–mid-May* ⇝ *31 rooms* ❖ *No Meals.*

 Activities

CAMPING
DeMotte Campground
CAMPGROUND | Surrounded by tall pines, this U.S. Forest Service campground is 25 miles south of Jacob Lake on Hwy. 67, just 7 miles before you get to the park's boundary. It has 38 single-unit (RV or tent) sites but no hookups, for $22. ✉ *Grand Canyon* ☎ *928/643–7395* ⊕ *www.recreation.gov* ⊗ *Closed Oct.–May.*

Kaibab Camper Village
CAMPGROUND | Firepits and more than 70 picnic tables are spread out in this wooded spot, which is near a gas station, store, and the restaurant at Jacob Lake Inn. Reservations are recommended, particularly during the height of the busy summer season. Although the campground is open May 14 through mid-October regardless, winter snow can delay the North Rim's opening or hasten its closure. ✉ *Grand Canyon* ☎ *928/643–7804* ⊕ *www. kaibabcampervillage.com* ⊗ *Closed mid-May–mid-October.*

Fredonia

72 miles from the North Rim entrance via Hwy. 89A and Hwy. 67.

Fredonia, a small community of about 1,300, approximately an hour's drive north of the Grand Canyon, is often referred to as the gateway to the North Rim; it's also relatively close to Zion and Bryce Canyon national parks in Utah and is just 7 miles from Kanab, Utah.

 Sights

Red Pueblo Museum
HISTORY MUSEUM | Located in a converted rest area, this small museum is packed with Native American artifacts found in the area and items early settlers left behind; you can also tour a collection of historic cabins and buildings. Usually, a docent or the owner himself is there to give a guided tour. Bring cash; the museum is free but relies on donations to keep going. ✉ *900 N. Hwy. 89A, Grand Canyon* ☎ *928/643–7777* ✉ *Free* ⊗ *Closed Sun.–Tues.*

🍽 Restaurants

Dining in Fredonia has a hard time competing with the more plentiful options in Kanab, Utah, just 7 miles north. The few offerings in Fredonia are mom-and-pop eateries and usually don't last long, but look for small Mexican restaurants, steak houses, and diners along Main Street, and you might get lucky. In Kanab, you'll find everything from white tablecloth fine dining to popular fast food chains. Whether you're driving through or staying in the area, you should plan on eating most, if not all, of your meals in Kanab.

🛏 Hotels

The lodging scene in Fredonia is similar to its dining scene; the community is overshadowed by its northern neighbor, Kanab, which has a plethora of chain hotels, historic properties, boutiques, and bed and breakfasts. Fredonia does have several cabins and single rooms available through vacation rental sites. If you want to stay in the area, you are probably better off looking at options in Kanab since this is where the restaurants are.

★ Bar 10 Ranch
$$$$ | **ALL-INCLUSIVE** | Wagon wheel chandeliers in the lodge, wood beam interiors, and 14 Conestoga covered wagons you can sleep in lend to the authentic Western vibe at Bar 10. **Pros:** sleep in a Conestoga covered wagon; lots of activities; beautiful, well-maintained property. **Cons:** very remote; no pets allowed; no cell phone service. *⑤ Rooms from: $290 ⊠ Grand Canyon ☎ 435/628–4010 ⊕ www.bar10.com ⊘ Closed mid-Nov.–mid-March. ⥅ 19 lodgings ⦿ All-Inclusive.*

🛍 Shopping

Homestead Tribal Arts
SOUVENIRS | This bright red store is crammed full of Native American jewelry, rugs, sculptures, pottery, and other traditional arts and crafts. You can find modern Native American art here, too, and a silversmith is on-site to repair jewelry. *⊠ 105 N. Main St., Grand Canyon ☎ 928/643–7287 ⊕ www.homesteadtribalarts.com.*

Marble Canyon

89 miles from the North Rim entrance via Hwy. 89A to U.S. 67.

Marble Canyon marks the geographical beginning of the Grand Canyon at its northeastern tip. It's a good stopping point if you're driving U.S. 89 to the North Rim. Anglers come from around the world to fish the waters of Lees Ferry just a few miles away in Glen Canyon Recreational Area.

Sights

SCENIC DRIVES
U.S. 89
SCENIC DRIVE | The route north from Cameron Trading Post on U.S. 89 offers a stunning view of the Painted Desert. The desert, which covers thousands of square miles stretching to the south and east, is a vision of subtle, almost harsh beauty, with windswept plains and mesas, isolated buttes, and barren valleys in pastel patterns. About 30 miles north of Cameron Trading Post, the Painted Desert country gives way to sandstone cliffs that run for miles. Brilliantly hued and ranging in color from light pink to deep orange, the Echo Cliffs rise to more than 1,000 feet in many places. They are essentially devoid of vegetation, but in a few high places, thick patches of tall cottonwood and poplar trees, nurtured by springs and water seepage from the rock escarpment, manage to thrive. ⊠ *Grand Canyon.*

U.S. 89A
SCENIC DRIVE | At Bitter Springs, 60 miles north of Cameron, U.S. 89A branches off from U.S. 89, running north and providing views of **Marble Canyon,** the geographical beginning of the Grand Canyon. Like the Grand Canyon, Marble Canyon was formed by the Colorado River. Traversing a gorge nearly 500 feet deep is **Navajo Bridge,** a narrow steel span built in 1929 and listed on the National Register of Historic Places. Formerly used for car traffic, it now functions only as a pedestrian overpass. ⊠ *Grand Canyon.*

SCENIC SPOTS
Vermilion Cliffs National Monument
NATURE SIGHT | West of the town of Marble Canyon are these spectacular cliffs, more than 3,000 feet high in many places. A four-wheel-drive vehicle is required here, as there are no paved roads and the sand is deep. Keep an eye out for condors; the giant endangered birds were reintroduced into the area in 1996. Reports suggest that the birds, once in captivity, are surviving well in the wilderness. ⊠ *Grand Canyon* ☎ *435/688–3200* ⊕ *www.blm. gov/node/10029.*

 Restaurants

Cliff Dwellers Restaurant

$$ | **AMERICAN** | At the end of a row of motel rooms at Cliff Dwellers Lodge, this restaurant is a pleasant surprise with excellent food, craft beer, and a full bar. Order gourmet sandwiches and salads for lunch; rib-eye steak, roasted chicken, and baby back ribs impress at dinner. **Known for:** full bar with craft beers and wines; avocado pie; patio dining with Vermillion Cliff views. $ *Average main: $20* ⊠ *Milepost 547 N. Hwy. 89A, Grand Canyon* ☎ *800/962–9755, 928/355–2261* ⊕ *cliffdwellerslodge.com.*

Hotels

Cliff Dwellers Lodge

$$ | **HOTEL** | Built in 1949, this dining and lodging complex sits at the foot of Vermilion Cliffs. **Pros:** very good on-site restaurant; two Tesla charging stations; pet-friendly. **Cons:** basic motel accommodations; not much in the area; no Wi-Fi. $ *Rooms from: $145* ⊠ *Milepost 547 N. Hwy. 89A, Grand Canyon* ☎ *800/962–9755, 928/355–2261* ⊕ *cliffdwellerslodge.com* ↝ *23 rooms* ⦿ *No Meals.*

Lee's Ferry Lodge

$$ | **HOTEL** | Originally built to house workers helping to construct the Navajo Bridge in the 1920s, this stone-faced motel has themed rooms and an on-site restaurant. **Pros:** closest accommodations to Lees Ferry; historic, 1920s-era property; clean, recently renovated rooms. **Cons:** motel-style lodge; not much going on in the area; no Wi-Fi. $ *Rooms from: $140* ⊠ *Milepost 5415 N. Hwy. 89A, Grand Canyon* ☎ *928/355–2231* ⊕ *vermilioncliffs.com* ↝ *11 rooms* ⦿ *No Meals.*

Marble Canyon Lodge

$$ | **HOTEL** | Popular with anglers and rafters, this lodge offers two types of accommodations: standard rooms in the original lodge building and two-bedroom apartments in a newer building. **Pros:** convenience store, restaurant, and trading post; great fishing on the Colorado River; some rooms have kitchens. **Cons:** no-frills rustic lodging; no Wi-Fi (one computer in lobby); apartments have evaporative coolers instead of air-conditioning. $ *Rooms from: $159* ⊠ *U.S. 89A, Grand Canyon* ✛ *¼ mile west of Navajo Bridge* ☎ *928/355–2225, 800/726–1789* ⊕ *www.marblecanyoncompany.com* ↝ *52 rooms* ⦿ *No Meals.*

Activities

BOATING AND RAFTING

The National Park Service authorizes 15 concessionaires to run rafting trips through the canyon—you can view a full list at the park's website (⊕ *www.nps.gov/grca/planyourvisit/river-concessioners.htm*). Trips run from 3 to 18 days, depending on whether you opt for the upper canyon, lower canyon, or full canyon, and whether you ride in motorized or nonmotorized rafts. You can also experience a one-day rafting trip, either running a few rapids in the Grand Canyon West with the Hualapai tribe or floating through Glen Canyon near Page in northeast Arizona.

Arizona Raft Adventures

WHITE-WATER RAFTING | This outfitter organizes 6- to 16-day paddle/oar and motor trips through the upper, lower, or full canyon, for all skill levels. ⊠ *4050 E. Huntington Dr., Grand Canyon* ☎ *800/786–7238, 928/526–8200* ⊕ *azraft.com* ✉ *From $2,645* ⊗ *Closed Nov.–Mar.*

Canyoneers

WHITE-WATER RAFTING | With a reputation for high quality and a roster of 4- to 14-day trips, Canyoneers is popular with those who want to do some hiking into side canyons as well. Motorized and oar trips are available mid-April through September. ⊠ *7195 N. U.S. 89, Grand Canyon* ☎ *928/526–0924, 800/525–0924* ⊕ *canyoneers.com* ✉ *From $2,025.*

Grand Canyon Expeditions

WHITE-WATER RAFTING | You can count on Grand Canyon Expeditions to take you down the Colorado River safely and in style: evening meals might include filet mignon, pork chops, or shrimp. The 8- or 9-day motorized and 14- or 16-day Dory trips cover all 277 miles of the river, and some trips focus on special interests like archaeology and photography. Round-trip transportation from Las Vegas is part of the package. ⊠ *Grand Canyon* ☎ *435/644–2691, 800/544–2691* ⊕ *www.gcex.com* ✉ *From $3,050.*

Wilderness River Adventures

WHITE-WATER RAFTING | One of the canyon's larger rafting outfitters, Wilderness River Adventures by Aramark runs a wide variety of trips from 3 to 14 days, oar or motorized, from April to September. Their most popular trip is the 7-day motorized trip. ⊠ *199 Kaibab Rd., Grand Canyon* ☎ *928/645–0343 Grand Canyon rafting, 928/645–6906 Horseshoe Bend rafting, 928/645–4967 Grand Canyon rafting* ⊕ *www.riveradventures.com* ✉ *From $1,600 (for 3-day trip).*

FISHING

The stretch of ice-cold, crystal clear water at Lees Ferry off the North Rim provides arguably the best trout fishing in the Southwest. Many rafters and anglers stay the night in a campground near the river or in nearby Marble Canyon before hitting the river at dawn.

Lees Ferry Anglers

FISHING | There are guides, state fishing licenses, and gear for sale at Lees Ferry Anglers. ⊠ *Milepost 547 N. U.S. 89A, Hwy. 67, Grand Canyon* ☎ *928/355–2261, 800/962–9755* ⊕ *www.leesferry. com.*

Lees Ferry on the Fly

FISHING | Guides take guests out on the Colorado River for a full day of both fly-fishing and spin fishing. Quality gear, including Orvis rods and reels, is provided if you don't have your own. ⊠ *Grand Canyon* ☎ *928/380–4504, 928/522–4124* ⊕ *leesferryon-thefly.com.*

Marble Canyon Outfitters

FISHING | This company, based at Marble Canyon Lodge, sells Arizona fishing licenses and offers top-notch guided fishing trips. ⊠ *Grand Canyon* ⊕ *¼ mile west of Navajo Bridge on U.S. 89A* ☎ *800/533–7339* ⊕ *www.leesferryflyfishing.com.*

HIKING
Rainbow Rim Trail

BIKING | Rangers say the best bet for bikers heading to the North Rim—and only intermediate and experienced ones should attempt it—is the Rainbow Rim Trail, an 18-mile, one-way trail that begins at Parissawampitts Point at the end of Forest Road 214 and ends at Timp Point on Forest Road 271. This premier trail outside the park boundary includes three fantastic viewpoints of the Grand Canyon—Fence, Locust, and North Timp—and winds through a ponderosa pine forest, aspen groves, and pristine meadows. In the Kaibab National Forest, the trail is open to hikers, bikers, and horseback riders and stays within 200 feet of its 7,550 feet elevation. ⊠ *Grand Canyon* ☎ *928/643–7395* ⊕ *www.fs.usda.gov/ kaibab.*

KAYAKING
Kayak the Colorado

KAYAKING | Rent kayaks, canoes, inflatable oar boats, paddleboats, and stand-up paddleboards to navigate the Colorado River for the day. Additional gear including sleeping pads and dry bags is available, too. ⊠ *Grand Canyon* ☎ *928/856–0012* ⊕ *www.kayakthecol-orado.com.*

Index

Photo Credits

Front Cover: Merrill Images/Getty Images [**Description:** United States, Arizona, Grand Canyon National Park, group paddling a whitewater raft on Colorado River.] **Back cover, from left to right:** Fellvred/Dreamstime. Skreidzeleu/Shutterstock. Diegograndi/iStockphoto. **Spine:** Lucky photographer/Shutterstock. **Interior, from left to right:** Skreidzeleu/Shutterstock (1).Serj Malomuzh/Shutterstock (2-3). **Chapter 1: Experience Grand Canyon National Park:** Pat Tr/Shutterstock (6-7). Blazekg/iStockphoto (8-9). Whit Richardson/Alamy (9). Raeann Davies/Shutterstock (9). Perseomedusa/Dreamstime (10). NPS Photo (10). Xanterra Travel Collection (10). Agafapaperiapunta/iStockphoto (10). Nootprapa/Shutterstock (11). Roman Khomlyak/Shutterstock (11). Sean Pavone/iStockphoto (12). NPS/Mark Lellouch (12). Edwin Verin/Shutterstock (13). Fblanco4/Dreamstime (18). Fellvred/Dreamstime (18). NPS Photo/J. Baird (18). NPS Photo/Andrew Cattoir (18). Serj Malomuzh/Shutterstock (19). Thenatureguy1/Dreamstime (19). Nikki Yancey/Shutterstock (19). Redwood8/Dreamstime (19). Tristanbnz/Dreamstime (20). TLF Images/Shutterstock (20). NPS (20). Georgi Baird/Shutterstock (20). Vaclav Sebek/Shutterstock (21). Rinusbaak/Dreamstime (21). Blue-Sky-Media/Shutterstock (21). James Marvin Phelps/Shutterstock (21). Nate Loper/Shutterstock (22). Christian_b/Shutterstock (22). ScenincMedia/Dreamstime (22). Christian_b/Shutterstock (22). Anton Foltin/Shutterstock (23). **Chapter 3: The South Rim:** Filip Fuxa/Shutterstock (47). Autumn Sky Photography/Shutterstock (55). Konoplytska/Shutterstock (58). Ventdusud/Shutterstock (60-61). Danielaphotography/Dreamstime (62). Roman Khomlyak/Shutterstock (64-65). Paul R. Jones/Shutterstock (72). Ron Greer/Shutterstock (79). Kerrick James/Grand Canyon National Park (81). **Chapter 4: The North Rim:** Sasha Buzko/Shutterstock (85). Kerrick James/Grand Canyon Lodge (91). Roman Khomlyak/Shutterstock (96-97). IrinaK/Shutterstock (104-105). **Chapter 5: The West Rim and Havasu Canyon:** Sandra Foyt/Shutterstock (107). Nootprapa/Shutterstock (114-115). Matt Fowler/iStockphoto (116). Iacomino Frimages/Shutterstock (122-123). Sandra Foyt/Shutterstock (127). Lightphoto/iStockphoto (128-129). **Chapter 6: Gateways:** A Hornung/Shutterstock (131). Supitchamcsdam/iStockphoto (143). Michael Landrum/Shutterstock (147). Dominic Jeanmaire/Shutterstock (149). Clairewhite03/Dreamstime (164). Don Graham/Wikimedia Commons (169). Kevin Oke Photo/Shutterstock (171). PT Hamilton/Shutterstock (172-173). **About Our Writers:** Teresa Bitler, courtesy of Rick D'Elia (192).

Every effort has been made to trace the copyright holders, and we apologize in advance for any accidental errors. We would be happy to apply the corrections in the following edition of this publication.

Notes

Notes

Notes

Notes